The Interview Answer

The Interview Answer

10 Essential Tips for Acing Your Job Interview

Patricia A. Flaherty

Dedicated to my family
with love and gratitude

Table of Contents

Preface

I come from a large family. With so many siblings, in-laws, sons, daughters, nieces, nephews, and cousins, multiple professions abound among us. Our ranks include doctors, lawyers, psychologists, engineers, bankers, educators, and more. I have always felt fortunate to have such a wealth of expert resources to draw upon in times of need.

My contribution to the group is as an educator and human resources (HR) professional, with over forty years of professional experience and multiple graduate and postgraduate degrees in related fields. My career began as a teacher, first in the classroom and then in the corporate setting. During the latter half of my career, I held senior corporate HR positions, including that of chief learning officer at such Fortune 100 companies as MCI and the Ford Motor Company. I recently retired from Ford, where I was the global director of both Ford Learning and Development and Ford HR Strategy. In these roles, I led professional development efforts for all Ford employees, from new hires to senior executives, and I helped develop the company-wide behaviors that Ford candidates are assessed against during the interview process. In retirement, I consulted with Ford on the creation of its best-in-class talent acquisition strategy. I continue to provide coaching, consulting, and volunteer services to both for-profit and not-for-profit organizations.

Throughout my career I have interviewed, been interviewed, and coached interviewers and interviewees countless times. So whenever my family members, friends, or colleagues are about to interview for a job, they tend to come to me for advice. In this book, I have distilled that advice into ten tips that are *essential* for acing your interview. I teach you what interviewers are looking for and how to *answer*—and *ask*—questions well. I also give you a rare peek into interviewers' minds so that you can clearly see how your words shape their impressions of you. The book is a quick read, with an easy, conversational style, multiple examples, and ample opportunities to practice. Its tips are equally applicable if you are being interviewed by one person at a time or simultaneously by a group/panel of interviewers.

The Interview Answer is intended for you as the "interviewee" (the person being interviewed); its starting point assumes that you have been contacted for an in-person, video, or telephone job interview. Although my primary focus is on helping *you* land the job you desire, these tips will also provide indirect guidance to an "interviewer" (the person conducting the interview).

This book does not cover how to create your résumé or how to go about the job search process. Similarly, it does not cover preinterview screening methods, such as assessment instruments (cognitive ability tests, personality inventories, and the like), or preinterview telephone screening. It strictly focuses on how to best answer and ask questions during your actual interview and how to increase your confidence and skills in order to be selected for the job you want.

Getting a job is a major life event and a significant achievement, particularly in a tough economy. Each job has the potential to provide you with financial security and to bring you a step closer to achieving your goals and aspirations. It is my sincere hope that these tips will help you increase your chances of landing the job you want and realizing your dreams.

I wish you the best of luck!

Know What Interviewers Are Looking (and Listening) For

What if you were taking an important college course, but you were not given the course syllabus at the beginning of the semester? The missing syllabus would have included exactly what you would be graded on and how those items would be weighed. Without that syllabus, imagine how disadvantaged you would be that semester. You would be unaware of the criteria the professor would be measuring you against, and you would be unsure of how to attain the best grades possible.

The same holds true for interviews. The interviewer is measuring you and giving you a "grade" based on your performance during the discussion. If you are blind to the criteria you are being assessed against as you enter an interview, you are tremendously disadvantaged during the interview, and you will be less likely to do your best than if you had been better prepared. It is therefore critical to understand what interviewers are looking and listening for before you engage in the interview process.

Even if they are not always consciously aware of it, interviewers are looking and listening for three major things about you during the interview process. I call these factors the "3 Cs": (1) Character, (2) Competence, and (3) Chemistry/compatibility.

1. CHARACTER

"Character" is defined by the attributes, qualities, and traits you possess, such as your integrity, honesty, loyalty, commitment, self-motivation, initiative, humility, positive attitude, and ability to be a team player. Your character is affected by your innate predispositions and the experiences of your formative years; it is strongly influenced by your family and cultural value systems.

Your character is usually solidly formed by the time you enter the job market, and it cannot easily be made or unmade in work settings or training sessions. It is therefore critical for the interviewer to try to assess your character during the interview process. Good interviewers know that the best chance they have to weed out interviewees with undesirable character traits (at least for the purposes of their companies) is during the selection process. This is because once people of poor character come aboard an organization, it is difficult to change them or work with them—or even to terminate them, should that become necessary. Good interviewers will therefore do their best to assess your character during the interview process.

You may wonder why I didn't list "competence" (see below) first. It's not that competence isn't just as important as character; you generally wouldn't even be at the interview in the first place unless your résumé showed that you had the basic competence to be considered. Still, most of us know of people who would be extremely competent (knowledgeable and skilled) for a particular job, yet we would not personally hire that person for a given job, nor would we recommend the person to a good friend. Why is that? It is often because the person does not have the character we believe would make him/her a good employee—either for ourselves or someone else.

2. COMPETENCE

By "competence," I mean the knowledge, skills, and abilities you have to do the job, based on your prior learning and experience and your intelligence. The competencies required for the job you are seeking are often listed in the position/job description.

Some of the knowledge and skills you have are transferrable. You can apply your transferrable competencies, such as business acumen, interpersonal skills, and oral and written communication skills, just about anywhere—in multiple organizations, functions within an organization, and jobs within a function. For example, if you have great written and oral communication skills, these skills can serve you just as well as a sales associate for General Electric or as a marketing analyst for Coca-Cola. Some of your other competencies are more organization, function, or job specific, and they may be unique to a given type of job or role. For example, you may have knowledge of a particular type of legal procedure or engineering process.

Employers are usually looking to see if you have many generic, transferrable skills and some unique, job-specific skills in place. The general and job-specific competencies an employer feels you must have are often listed as being "required" in the position description. The competencies that employers would like you to have but may be willing to help you develop are often listed as being "preferred" on the position description.

Your competence is very important to employers. It indicates how qualified you are to perform the job that they are filling. The more knowledgeable you are about how to do the job, the faster you can get past the learning curve and become a productive employee.

In some cases, a certain level of demonstrated competence is required for you to even get an interview—for example, possessing nursing experience or a certain number of years playing in an orchestra. Many interviews have a "technical" component during which interviewers try to assess your competence in depth; they sometimes even ask you to demonstrate that competence (for example, by playing an instrument or taking a test). Even if it is only assessed via the interviewer's questions, however, your competence is always being looked for (and listened for) during the interview process.

3. CHEMISTRY/COMPATIBILITY

"Chemistry/compatibility" refers to the degree of affinity, attraction, and rapport you have with the people who interview you. People like to work with people they like; they want to work with people whom they can see themselves (and others) working with well. During an interview, even if it's only subconsciously, interviewers assess how you will interact with them and their colleagues—and whether they and their colleagues will be able to (or will want to) work with you. They will decide how well you will "fit" in their organization and how well suited you will be to its culture.

Although the third of the "3 Cs" is not as tangible or concrete as the other two, it is still important. In order to understand the importance of chemistry/compatibility, recall some of the people you have dated in the past. Perhaps some of them were good looking, smart (competent), and even had good character. But if you didn't have any chemistry/compatibility with them, how likely were you to go out with them again—let alone marry them?

In the final analysis, interviewers will decide if they think you are someone whom they will ask to "marry" into their organization. So, establishing rapport and some sort of a connection or chemistry/compatibility with your interviewer is essential.

NOW YOU TRY IT!

To test your understanding of what is meant by character, competence, and chemistry/compatibility (the "3 Cs"), place the following words and phrases into the appropriate columns of the table below. Try to find the best fit, and place no more than two words or phrases in each category.

- Integrity
- Engineering knowledge
- Congeniality
- Typing skills
- Likability
- Honesty

Character	Competence	Chemistry/Compatibility
•	•	•
•	•	•

WHAT DO YOU THINK?

How did you do? Did you place "integrity" and "honesty" in the character category? And did you put "engineering knowledge" and "typing skills" in the competence category? Finally, although "congeniality" and "likeability" could be considered character traits, did you see that they fit best in the chemistry/compatibility category? If so, you are well on your way to understanding the 3 Cs.

SUMMARY: TIP 1

It is important to understand what an interviewer is looking and listening for before you engage in the interview process. A good interviewer is consciously or unconsciously looking and listening for your 3 Cs during your interview—your character, competence, and chemistry/compatibility.

"Character" refers to the attributes, qualities, and traits that are ingrained in you. It is critical for interviewers to assess your character during interviews, because they cannot teach it or change it after they've hired you.

"Competence" refers to the knowledge, skills, and abilities you have, based on your prior learning and experience and your intelligence. Your competence is also critically important to an interviewer, because it reflects your qualifications for the job as well as the degree of the learning curve required for you to become a fully productive employee. Your competencies include those that you can transfer across multiple positions and those that are unique to a given position. Your potential employer may consider some competencies to be required and others to be preferred. He/she may be willing to help you develop some of the preferred competencies after you are hired.

Finally, interviewers will also look for your chemistry/compatibility during the interview process. Although this factor is more intangible than the other two, interviewers will try to assess if you are someone they and others will be able to get along with and if you are a person whom they believe will fit well within their organizational culture.

Tip Two

Understand Behavioral Event Interviewing

If character, competence, and chemistry/compatibility are the three things interviewers look for, how do they find out if you have these qualities? Simply put, they do this by asking you—and by listening intently to your answers. Good interviewers listen more than they talk, which unfortunately is a skill that not all interviewers have mastered. Their primary role is to ask you good open-ended questions and to listen deeply to your answers (with their eyes as well as their ears) for indicators of the 3 Cs noted above.

Your interviewer may ask you many types of questions. Some of these questions may be simple and straightforward ("Why do you want this job?"). Other questions may be more complex and will require you to tell a story. This latter type of questioning technique, which may be used at various points during your interview, is called "behavioral event interviewing," or BEI.

BEHAVIORAL EVENT INTERVIEWING

BEI is a type of open-ended questioning that asks you to describe different events (situations) in your past, how you handled them (behavior), and what the outcomes (results) were. In past-focused scenarios, interviewers ask you, "What *did* you do [in the past]" in order to determine "What *will* you do [in the future]?" if they hire you. This strategy is based on the premise that *your past behavior is the greatest predictor of your future behavior.*

Interviewers will probe to understand your 3 Cs via the questions they ask you. The person who has the most control of how your 3 Cs are perceived is *you*—by your answers to the interviewer's questions. For this reason, understanding the types of questions you will be asked (including BEI-type questions) and how to answer them well is important for a successful interview.

EXAMPLE 2–1

Let's take a nonprofessional example to illustrate this point. Suppose a person was planning to make a bet on one of two runners who were about to begin training for an upcoming race. The person making the bet (the "bettor") was asked to do so before the two runners began training; the bettor stood to win a large sum of money if the contestant whom he/she wagered on won the race. Before selecting the contestant to wager on, the bettor was given the chance to interview both contestants and to ask them one question. If the bettor was using the BEI technique, that question might be something like this (emphasis added): "Tell me about a time when you had to train for a race. What was the *situation*, how did you go about it (*behavior*), and what were the *results*?"

With this technique, the person placing the wager is asking the contestants to describe their behavior and results in past situations in order to predict their behavior and results in future situations. If the contestants answer well, the bettor will feel more comfortable placing a wager on their success in the upcoming race. Likewise, if the contestants do not answer well, the bettor will feel less comfortable placing a wager on their success.

Let's look again at the question the bettor asked (using the BEI technique). This time, let's also look at the answer each contestant provided to the bettor's question. We'll call the contestants Contestant A and Contestant B.

BETTOR'S QUESTION

Tell me about a time when you had to train for a race. What was the situation, how did you go about it, and what were the results?

ANSWER: CONTESTANT A

Well, once I was training for a 5K, and my goal was to cross the finish line in under twenty minutes. I meant to go running every day to prepare for it, but I got pretty busy with school and personal stuff, so I was only able to train about twice a week. I didn't think that would be a problem, though, because I'm just naturally gifted at running, and I figured two days of training a week would be OK for someone like me.

At one point, I pulled a tendon, and my doctor said it was because I didn't do any stretching before or after I ran. I wish somebody had told me that beforehand. In the end, I completed the race, but my time was twenty-two minutes, which was OK, because it put me about in the middle of the pack. The person who won finished the race in eighteen minutes and thirty seconds.

ANSWER: CONTESTANT B

Last year, I was training for a triathlon, which had running, swimming, and biking segments. I had always wanted to push myself to see if I could do a triathlon and to try to finish in the top three. Even though I've been active in sports all my life, I knew this would require a lot of training.

The running segment of the triathlon was 5K in distance. My personal goal was to run that segment in (at the most) twenty minutes.

Although it was sometimes hard to find the time, I trained daily without fail, making sure to increase the speed and lengths of my runs gradually and to pay attention to warm-up and cool-down stretching in order to prevent injury as best I could. I ended up beating my personal goal in the running segment by doing it in eighteen minutes. And that time helped me come in second in the entire triathlon.

INSIDE THE MIND OF THE BETTOR

Now put yourself inside the mind of the bettor. What do these answers lead the bettor to think about each of the candidates? Look at the table below for examples of what the interviewer might be thinking about Contestant A's character, competence, and chemistry/compatibility based on Contestant A's answer.

Bettor's Question: *Tell me about a time when you had to train for a race. What was the situation, how did you go about it, and what were the results?*

Answer: Contestant A

Well, once I was training for a 5K, and my goal was to cross the finish line in under twenty minutes. I meant to go running every day to prepare for it, but I got pretty busy with school and personal stuff, so I was only able to train about twice a week. I didn't think that would be a problem, though, because I'm just naturally gifted at running, and I figured two days of training a week would be OK for someone like me.

At one point, I pulled a tendon, and my doctor said it was because I didn't do any stretching before or after I ran. I wish somebody had told me that beforehand. In the end, I completed the race, but my time was twenty-two minutes, which was OK, because it put me about in the middle of the pack. The person who won finished the race in eighteen minutes and thirty seconds.

Interviewer's Thoughts		
Character	**Competence**	**Chemistry/Compatibility**
Does this contestant not have perseverance? When things get tough, will this contestant make excuses and not find a way to accomplish the task at hand? Is this contestant egocentric with an inflated opinion of him/herself? Will this contestant think that he/she does not need to put in the work required for a task and that it will be OK to just coast on natural abilities? Does this contestant like to blame others when things go wrong? Will he/she not take personal accountability for his/her decisions? Does this contestant not really care about achieving the goal he/she set out to achieve? Will this contestant be comfortable settling for mediocre performance?	Does this contestant not know the basics of running and how to warm up properly? Will this contestant not be prepared with even the fundamental knowledge required?	Will this contestant's ego and inflated opinion of him/herself make him/her difficult to work with? Will this contestant's tendency to blame others for his/her own decisions or issues create tension and bad feelings with others?

INSIDE THE MIND OF THE BETTOR

Now let's go back inside the mind of the bettor as he/she listens to Contestant B's answer. Let's look at the table below for some possible interviewer thoughts about Contestant B's character, competence, and chemistry/compatibility, based on Contestant B's answer.

Bettor's Question: *Tell me about a time when you had to train for a race. What was the situation, how did you go about it, and what were the results?*

Answer: Contestant B

Last year, I was training for a triathlon, which had running, swimming, and biking segments. I had always wanted to push myself to see if I could do a triathlon and to try to finish in the top three. Even though I've been active in sports all my life, I knew this would require a lot of training.

The running segment of the triathlon was 5K in distance. My personal goal was to run that segment in (at the most) twenty minutes.

Although it was sometimes hard to find the time, I trained daily without fail, making sure to increase the speed and lengths of my runs gradually and to pay attention to warm-up and cool-down stretching in order to prevent injury as best I could. I ended up beating my personal goal in the running segment by doing it in eighteen minutes. And that time helped me come in second in the entire triathlon.

Interviewer's Thoughts		
Character	**Competence**	**Chemistry/Compatibility**
Wow. A triathlon. That takes a lot of work. And he/she set out to finish in the top three. This seems to be a contestant who will be willing to push him/herself to achieve stretch goals and strive for peak performance. This contestant seems to be a person who will be humble enough not to rest on past accomplishments when seeking to achieve future goals. This contestant seems to be the kind of person who will show perseverance even in challenging circumstances. And he/she will be proactive about taking measures to avoid potential pitfalls. This contestant seems to be the kind of person who will achieve or beat the goals he/she sets for him/herself.	This contestant is knowledgeable enough to know that it will require a lot of training to achieve success. This contestant is educated about the warm-up, cool-down, and pacing regimens required to train properly and prevent injury. This contestant is a skilled athlete with proven results.	This contestant would be a pleasure to work with and would positively influence others with his/her great work ethic.

WHAT DO YOU THINK?

Do you see how someone can gain insight into a candidate's character, competence, and chemistry/compatibility by asking a BEI-type question? And do you see where that insight comes from?

Let's say you are Contestant A. How do you think you did, based on your answer to the BEI-type question? What impression did your answer give the bettor about your degree of self-discipline and persistence (character traits), knowledge of training techniques (competence), and probable rapport between yourself and others (chemistry/compatibility)? Based on your answer, how positively or negatively do you think you were perceived by the bettor? And who gave the bettor those perceptions? *You* did.

Now let's say you are Contestant B. How do you think you did, based on your answer to the BEI-type question? What impression did your answer give the bettor about your work ethic and achievement orientation (character traits), athletic knowledge and skill (competence), and probable relationships with others (chemistry/compatibility)? Based on your answer, how positively or negatively do you think you were perceived by the bettor? And who gave the interviewer those perceptions? *You* did.

Clearly, the bettor would be more favorably impressed by Contestant B and in turn would be more willing to place a wager that Contestant B would win the race.

This is exactly what happens during an interview for a professional position. The interviewer is the bettor. He/she is trying to decide whether or not to "bet" (place his/her company's money) on you. Just as in the above example, real interviewers would be more likely to place a "bet" on a candidate who answers BEI-type questions well during a professional interview. By using BEI-type questions, interviewers try to assess the character, competence, and chemistry/compatibility that you have shown in past situations in order to determine whether or not they would feel comfortable betting the company's money on your success in future situations.

Here is another example of a BEI-type question:

- *Tell me about a situation when you were faced with conflicting priorities.* (Situation)

- *What did you do to determine your top priority?* (Behavior)
- *And what happened as a result?* (Results)

Again, you can see the three-part structure of the question: situation, behavior, and results.

Interviewers may not use the exact words "situation," "behavior," and "results" when they ask BEI-type questions. A question may be phrased something like, "Describe for me a time when you had to work with a difficult teammate. How did you handle that? And how did everything turn out?" Still, you can see the three parts of the question:

- *Describe for me a time when you had to work with a difficult teammate.* (Situation)
- *How did you handle that?* (Behavior)
- *And how did everything turn out?* (Results)

It is important to note that not all BEI-type questions clearly call out all three parts of the structure. Some questions require that you tell the interviewer about what may seem to be only a *situation*. Consider this example:
Tell me about a time when you had to use project management skills.

The BEI-type questions mentioned previously could also have been asked in that same way, as follows:

- *Tell me about a situation when you were faced with conflicting priorities.*
- *Describe for me a time when you had to work with a difficult teammate.*

In these cases, although it may seem like the interviewers are only asking you to describe the *situations*, they also want you to include your *behaviors* and *results* in your answers. It is always important to address all three parts of a BEI-type question, even when they are not explicitly called out.

Some people use acronyms to help them remember the three parts of a BEI-type question, such as "car": context, action, and results (which would translate to our examples as situation, behavior, and results, respectively). Feel free to use whichever words and acronyms are most helpful to you, as long as they help you to recognize and address the three parts of a BEI-type question.

As mentioned at the beginning of this chapter, not all interview questions are BEI-type questions. Since BEI-type questions are frequently used during the interview process, however, it is wise to learn how to recognize them and answer them well. And remember, no matter what kind of questions they may ask, interviewers are always looking (and listening) for your 3 Cs in your answer.

EXAMPLE 2–2

Although this book primarily concentrates on what you *say* during an interview, you will also need to keep in mind that what you *do* in an interview can be just as telling to an interviewer. Sometimes, those actions can speak even louder than words.

To illustrate this idea, let's use an example in which two people, whom we'll call Candidate A and Candidate B, are both applying for the same job. In this example, what would it tell the interviewer if Candidate A arrives late for the interview, chews gum noisily, and dresses inappropriately? And what would it tell the interviewer if Candidate B arrives on time (or even a bit early) for the interview, does not chew gum, and dresses appropriately?

Let's use the table again to help us get inside the mind of the interviewer and to see what he/she might be thinking about these two candidates.

INSIDE THE MIND OF THE INTERVIEWER

	Interviewer's Thoughts		
	Character	**Competence**	**Chemistry/Compatibility**
Candidate A • Arrives late • Chews gum noisily • Dresses inappropriately	This candidate does not seem to be a punctual person. Is this candidate the kind of person who will not be responsible and respectful?	Does this candidate not have the type of business knowledge or social acumen to recognize what is appropriate for the occasion?	Is this candidate the kind of person I want to work with and want others in this organization to work with? Would he/she set an unprofessional example?
Candidate B • Arrives on time (or a little bit early) • Does not chew gum • Dresses very appropriately	This candidate seems to be a punctual person. This candidate gives the impression of being responsible and respectful.	This candidate seems to have the business knowledge and social acumen to recognize what is appropriate for the occasion.	This candidate demonstrates the kind of professionalism that I like on my team.

WHAT DO YOU THINK?

Given these behaviors and the perceptions that such behaviors create about the candidates' character, competence, and chemistry/compatibility, which candidate do you think the interviewer would be more apt to hire? And, if you were one of those candidates, who do you think had the most power to influence the interviewer's perceptions? *You* did.

SUMMARY: TIP 2

Skilled interviewers try to assess your character, competence, and chemistry/compatibility during interviews by asking you many open-ended questions and listening intently to your answers. Some interview questions are simple and straightforward, while others are more complex and require that you tell a story. This latter type of questioning technique, which will likely be used at various points during your interview, is called "Behavioral Event Interviewing" or BEI. BEI is a type of open-ended questioning technique that asks you to describe different events (situations) in your past, how you handled them (behavior), and what happened as a result (results). It is based upon the premise that *your past behavior is the greatest predictor of your future behavior.*

You are the person who most influences the interviewer's perceptions of your 3 Cs. By understanding BEI-type questions and what an interviewer is looking (and listening) for in your answers (and behaviors), you can more positively influence the interviewer's perceptions of you and strengthen your candidacy for the position you want.

Tip Three

Realize That It's Not All about You

This is one of the most counterintuitive yet important pieces of advice found in this book. When you go to an interview, it is understandable that you might think that it is supposed to be all about *you*. After all, it is *your* job, *your* life, and *yourself* that you are talking about. Especially if you possess critical and in-demand skills, you may be tempted to think that the sole focus should be what your potential employer can do for *you*.

That is not true, however. It is also about what you can do for the organization you are interviewing with: how you can contribute to *their* goals, *their* work, and *their* success. It is also about *them* and what you can do for *them*.

During the interview process, until you get a written offer (see the epilogue for more on this), you are the "seller," and the interviewer is the "buyer." The product you are selling is *you*.

Think of a product that someone might try to sell you; let's say it is a sports car. How might the seller pitch the product to you, the buyer? What if the seller tried to get you to buy the product by telling you how great it would be for him/her if you bought it? That pitch might sound something like this:

If you buy this sports car, I would make a large commission off of you, which would allow me take a nice vacation. My family would really like that. It would also really help my company achieve its sales goals and become more profitable. And if my company is profitable, I might even get a bonus this year.

Who is that pitch all about? The seller—not the buyer. And how likely would you, the buyer, be to consider buying that product based on that sales pitch? Not very likely, I would guess.

Good sellers know that the way to sell a product is not to make it about themselves, but about the buyer—and what the product can do for the buyer. A buyer-focused sales pitch for that same product might sound something like this:

If you buy this sports car, it will give you a sense of freedom and command of the road. You'll have lots of fun and will be the envy of all your friends. You'll also get great gas mileage, and you'll have a high-quality vehicle that will last for years. And I'll even throw in a five-year warranty so that you won't have any parts or service charges to worry about.

Now how likely would you be to consider buying the product based on that sales pitch? Certainly more than you would be from the first pitch.

This is the same situation you face in an interview. As mentioned, during the interview, you are the seller (selling yourself as the product), and the interviewer is the buyer. Most everything you say and ask should be about what you can do for *them* and not what *they* can do for *you*. Because, as strange as it may sound, it's not all about *you*.

EXAMPLE 3-1
Let's use a real example with a typical interview question to illustrate this point. Suppose two candidates are interviewing for a psychologist position with a not-for-profit organization that is dedicated to helping children of underprivileged families.

INTERVIEWER'S QUESTION
Why are you interested in this position?

ANSWER: CANDIDATE A
I would like to use my master's degree in psychology and my clinical experience to help young children maximize their potential and overcome the obstacles presented

to them by challenging environments. I believe in the mission of this organization and its commitment to the welfare of every child, and I would be proud to lend my talents to advancing this worthy goal.

ANSWER: CANDIDATE B

I have a master's degree in psychology, and I need a certain number of clinical hours to maintain my certification. This job would provide me with those hours when I meet your clients. I would like to help with the good work of this organization, and the job would also provide me with the income I need to pay off some of my student loans.

INSIDE THE MIND OF THE INTERVIEWER

Now let's go back inside the mind of the interviewer to see how the candidates' answers shown in the example above might influence the interviewer's thoughts about the candidates' 3 Cs and who or what each candidate is focused on serving (him/herself or the organization).

Interviewer's Question: *Why are you interested in this position?*		
Answer: Candidate A		
I would like to use my master's degree in psychology and my clinical experience to help young children maximize their potential and overcome the obstacles presented to them by challenging environments. I believe in the mission of this organization and its commitment to the welfare of every child, and I would be proud to lend my talents to advancing this worthy goal.		
Interviewer's Thoughts		
Character	**Competence**	**Chemistry/Compatibility**
This candidate values serving others above him/herself. This candidate is the kind of person who will dedicate him/herself to working for the welfare of our clients.	This candidate has the knowledge and advanced degree in psychology we need for this position. This candidate knows and understands the mission of our organization.	This candidate is exactly the kind of person I want to work with and want others in this organization to work with.

Interviewer's Question: *Why are you interested in this position?*		
Answer: Candidate B		
I have a master's degree in psychology, and I need a certain number of clinical hours to maintain my certification. This job would provide me with those hours when I meet with your clients. I would like to help with the good work of this organization, and the job would also provide me with the income I need to pay off some of my student loans.		
Interviewer's Thoughts		
Character	**Competence**	**Chemistry/Compatibility**
Is this candidate a self-centered person? Will he/she only work for his/her own benefit? Is this candidate only mildly interested in the needs of our organization and our clients, or is he/she primarily interested in using us to serve his/her own needs?	This candidate has the knowledge and advanced degree in psychology we need for this position.	Do we really want a person like this in our organization? Would this type of "me first" attitude make him/her difficult to work with and a poor team player?

WHAT DO YOU THINK?

Let's say you are Candidate A. What do you think of your answer? And *who* or *what* do you think your answer is about? You're right—it's about *their organization*. Your answer is about what hiring you could do for *them*. Like the car salesperson who talked about the fun and gas mileage the car would give the *buyer*, you are talking about what you would do for them (the buyer) and those they serve if they hired you for the position.

On the other hand, let's say you are Candidate B. What do you think of your answer? And *who* or *what* do you think your answer is about? You guessed it—it's about *you*. Your answer is about what hiring you could do for *you*. Just like the car salesperson who talked about the commission and bonus the *seller* would receive, you are talking about what the job could do for you (the seller) if they hired you for the position.

Based on these answers, which candidate do you think would be more likely to get the job? Candidate A, of course. And if you were one of those candidates, who do you think most influenced that decision? *You* did.

Once you insert yourself into the mind of the interviewer, it is easy to see how Candidate A's answer provides an advantage over Candidate B's answer. These answers also offer an example of how character can trump competence in an interview, particularly when competence is fairly equal among the different candidates. In this situation, both candidates have the knowledge and advanced degree in psychology that are required for the position. Yet Candidate A has the advantage over Candidate B, primarily because of what his/her answer indicates about his/her character (service-oriented, focused on helping others, etc.).

NOW YOU TRY IT!

Now that you've got the idea, think of a job you may someday be interested in applying for. Then try answering the following typical BEI-type interview question in a way that is not entirely about *you*, but about what *you* can do for *them*. (Remember that you are the seller and not the buyer.) Make sure to be mindful of what your answer will lead the interviewer to think about your character, competence, and chemistry/compatibility.

INTERVIEWER'S QUESTION
Why should we hire you for this job?

YOUR ANSWER

_____

_____

_____

_____

INSIDE THE MIND OF THE INTERVIEWER

Now try putting yourself inside the mind of the interviewer. Copy your answer into the table below. Based on your answer, jot down what you think the interviewer's thoughts might be about your character, competence, and chemistry/compatibility, including who or what the interviewer might think you are primarily focused on serving (*you* or *them*).

Interviewer's Question: *Why should we hire you for this job?*		
Your Answer:		
Interviewer's Thoughts		
Character	**Competence**	**Chemistry/Compatibility**

WHAT DO YOU THINK?

Based on your answer, how positively or negatively do you think you influenced the interviewer? Why do you think this? And who or what was your answer primarily about—*you*, and what they can do for *you*? Or *them*, and what you can do for *them*?

_____

_____

_____

_____

SUMMARY: TIP 3

Although it seems counterintuitive, your answers to interview questions should not be all about *you* and what the employer or job can do for *you*. Your answers should be about the organization and job (*them*) and what you can do for *them*. Until you get a written offer (see the epilogue for more on this), you are the "seller," and the interviewer is the "buyer." A good seller always focuses on what he/she can do for the buyer, and not the other way around.

So remember, as strange as it may sound, during the interview process, it really is *not all about you.*

Do Your Homework

Doing your homework means finding out as much information as possible about the hiring organization and about the position itself in advance of the interview. It also means reflecting on the ways in which your background and experiences meet the position's requirements, and it means taking the time to contemplate potential interview questions and practicing your answers ahead of time.

Most of us have had the experience of walking into a test, speech, meeting, sporting match, or other event where we should have been well prepared, but we were not. Even if we got lucky and the results were not disastrous, we knew in our hearts that the results could have been better if we had simply done our homework beforehand. The same holds true for interviews. If you really want to succeed in getting a job offer, you cannot rely on luck alone. Doing your homework in advance of an interview provides you with the ability to impress your interviewer with your proactivity, preparedness, and organizational knowledge. It also increases your confidence, skill level, and polish during the interview.

ORGANIZATIONAL INFORMATION

You can usually find a wealth of information about the hiring organization before your interview. Great sources for that information include the organization's website, published articles about the organization, the organization's annual reports, Internet searches about the organization, and people who are familiar with or have worked for the organization.

Such research can provide you with valuable information about the organization's history, vision, mission, markets, locations, products, services, profitability, strengths, challenges, culture, values, management, employees, business plans, and much more.

POSITION INFORMATION

Your best source of information about the position you are applying for is the position/job description. This is the piece of research that people most often overlook when preparing for an interview, yet it can be critical to their success.

Having the position description is like having the study guide (if not the answer key) to a test. Imagine that an instructor gave you the study guide to an important test, and you failed to study it beforehand. Wouldn't you feel silly—not to mention disadvantaged—when the time came to take the test? The same is true for studying the position description.

In the position description, you are being told exactly what requirements— qualifications, experience, knowledge, skills (competence), and attributes (character/compatibility)—the interviewer will be listening for in your answers. This information enables you to reflect on the ways in which you meet those requirements. It also provides you with advance insight on what questions you may be asked and the key messages you should try to highlight during your interview.

PRACTICE

The best way to practice for your interview is to anticipate the kinds of questions you may be asked, formulate your answers to those questions, and then rehearse your answers with another person—or even with yourself.

As mentioned above, the position description can provide you with insight into the kinds of questions you may be asked during your interview. Since some of those questions may be BEI-like in structure (asking you to describe situations, behaviors, and results), try to spend some time before your interview thinking of situations in your past that relate to the requirements listed in the position description. For example, if the position description calls for someone who has strong teamwork skills, prepare a few answers about situations in which you displayed great teamwork abilities. Practicing these answers with a friend or even in front of a mirror will help increase your confidence and skill (and the smoothness of your delivery) when interview time comes.

EXAMPLE 4–1

In order to illustrate how helpful doing your homework can be, let's use an example that shows the value of doing *organizational information* research in advance of your interview. In this example, let's suppose you are applying for a position with Johnson & Johnson, and you are asked the following interview question.

INTERVIEWER'S QUESTION

Why do you want to work for Johnson & Johnson?

YOUR ANSWER

I would be proud to work for this company, not only for its extensive product port-folio—from Band-Aids to medical diagnostics—and its year-over-year revenue and profitability growth but also because I believe in its Credo and its commitment to "protecting people first and property second."

Some companies espouse those values, but Johnson & Johnson actually lives by them. This was clearly seen in the 1982 Tylenol tampering crisis, when the company pulled all Tylenol products off the shelves and stopped all advertising (at a loss of a hundred million dollars) in order to ensure public safety. It then became the first company to comply with the Food and Drug Administration's request for tamper-resistant packaging.

These values are strongly aligned with my own, and I would consider it an honor to be part of such a company.

INSIDE THE MIND OF THE INTERVIEWER

Now put yourself inside the mind of the interviewer. What does your answer make the interviewer think about you as a candidate? Let's look at the table below for a glimpse of what the interviewer might be thinking about your character, competence, and chemistry/compatibility, based on your answer.

Interviewer's Question: *Why do you want to work for Johnson & Johnson?*

Your Answer:

I would be proud to work for this company, not only for its extensive product portfolio—from Band-Aids to medical diagnostics—and its year-over-year revenue and profitability growth, but also because I believe in its Credo and its commitment to "protecting people first and property second."

Some companies espouse those values, but Johnson & Johnson actually lives by them. This was clearly seen in the 1982 Tylenol tampering crisis, when the company pulled all Tylenol products off the shelves and stopped all advertising (at a loss of a hundred million dollars) in order to ensure public safety. It then became the first company to comply with the Food and Drug Administration's request for tamper-resistant packaging.

These values are strongly aligned with my own, and I would consider it an honor to be part of such a company.

Interviewer's Thoughts

Character	Competence	Chemistry/Compatibility
I'm impressed. This candidate certainly shows proactivity and a good work ethic by the degree of preparation he/she has clearly done for this interview. This candidate's values (people first, integrity, etc.) seem to be a good match with our own.	This candidate seems to have a good knowledge base about our company, our product line, our Credo, and our history. This candidate demonstrates good research skills.	This candidate seems to want to work for our company for reasons that would make him/her a good fit on our team.

WHAT DO YOU THINK?

Based on your answer, and the interviewer's thoughts, how well do you think you impressed the interviewer? Why do you think this? How did your answer demonstrate that you had done your homework beforehand?

NOW YOU TRY IT!

Think of an organization that you are currently applying to or would like to apply to someday. Do some research on the organization, and then try your hand at answering the question below. Fill in the blank with the name of the organization you have selected.

INTERVIEWER'S QUESTION

Why do you want to work at _____?

YOUR ANSWER

_____

_____

_____

_____

INSIDE THE MIND OF THE INTERVIEWER

Now, put yourself inside the mind of the interviewer. Copy your answer into the table below. Then try your hand at capturing the interviewer's thoughts about your character, competence, and chemistry/compatibility, based on your answer.

Interviewer's Question: *Why do you want to work at* _____ *? (Fill in the blank)*		
Your Answer:		
Interviewer's Thoughts		
Character	**Competence**	**Chemistry/Compatibility**

WHAT DO YOU THINK?

How do you think doing your homework beforehand influenced the interviewer's thinking? Based on your answer, how positively or negatively do you think the interviewer perceived you as a candidate?

_____

_____

_____

_____

SUMMARY: TIP 4

Just as you would prepare for any important event (a test, speech, sporting match, etc.) in order to do your best, it is important to do some homework in advance of your interview. This means finding out as much as possible about the hiring organization and the position itself beforehand. It also means taking the time to contemplate potential interview questions and to practice your answers ahead of time.

Organizational information includes the organization's history, vision, mission, markets, locations, products, services, profitability, strengths, challenges, culture, values, management, employees, business plans, and more. You can find that information in such sources as the organization's website, published articles about the organization, the organization's annual reports, Internet searches about the organization, and people who are familiar with or have worked for the organization.

Position information means the position requirements: qualifications, experience, knowledge, skills (competence), and attributes (character/compatibility). The best source of information about the position you are applying for is the position/job description, which will tell you exactly what the interviewer will be listening for in your answers. Studying the position description in advance of your interview is like reviewing the study guide (if not the answer key) to a test before you take it.

Practice involves anticipating the kinds of questions you may be asked and then formulating and rehearsing your potential answers (with a friend or in front of a mirror) ahead of time. The position description provides you with valuable clues about what questions you may be asked and what key messages you should try to highlight in your answers.

Doing your homework in advance of an interview gives you the ability to impress your interviewer with your proactivity, preparedness, and organizational knowledge. It also increases your confidence and skill level (and the smoothness of your delivery) when interview time comes.

INTRODUCTION TO TIPS 5–8: TELL YOUR STORY WELL

Now that you know what interviewers look for, the kinds of questioning techniques they use to find out if you have what they want, and the importance of doing your homework before the interview, let's discuss how you tell your story when answering an interview question.

You may wonder what I mean by the word "story." Storytelling comes into play when you answer just about any type of interview question, and it always comes into play when you answer a BEI-type question.

To refresh your memory from Tip 2, a BEI-type question asks you to describe the beginning, middle, and end of a scenario you have experienced in your past. The interviewer wants to know about the *situation* you were in, what your *behavior* was during that situation, and the *results* of that situation. In other words, the interviewer is asking you to tell the "story" of that experience, in three parts.

An example of this was shown in Tip 2, with the case of the two runners. In that case, the interviewer said, "Tell me about a time when you had to train for a race. What was the situation, how did you go about it, and what were the results?" You can easily see the three-part structure of that question: situation, behavior, and results.

It is important to note that not all BEI-type questions clearly call out the three parts of the structure. Some require that you tell the interviewer about what seems to be only a "situation" (for example, "Tell me about a time when you had a difficult assignment"). In these cases, the interviewer is still looking for you to include your behavior and results in your answer.

In addition, while not all interview questions are BEI-type questions (such as "Why do you want this job?"), bear in mind that whatever type of question you are asked and however it is phrased, you are still telling your story when you provide your answer.

We have all heard stories that are engaging, informative, and pleasing to hear, just as we have all heard stories that are painful, boring, and distressing to sit through. When telling your story during an interview, it is important to tell it in a way that showcases you and your history in the most favorable light.

Interviewers listen for indicators of your character, competence, and chemistry/compatibility as you tell your story. These indicators create a portrait of who you are to a potential employer. Before your interview, that portrait is a fairly blank canvas. During the interview, your portrait is created by the stories you tell. Because *you* are the painter who creates that portrait, it is important to tell your story well.

TIPS FOR TELLING YOUR STORY WELL

Now that you know how important the *way* you tell your story is to your interviewer's assessment of you, the next challenge is to learn *how* you can tell your story well. Of course, you must fully answer the interviewers' questions, no matter what questioning technique(s) they may use.

What else should you focus on (or not focus on)? If you are creating a self-portrait with your answers, what tips will help you paint yourself in the most favorable light? Tips 5–8 are all essential to telling your story well, as follows:

Tip 5: Tell Your Story Well, Part A: Be Concise

Tip 6: Tell Your Story Well, Part B: Highlight Key Messages

Tip 7: Tell Your Story Well, Part C: Mind Your Attitude

Tip 8: Tell Your Story Well, Part D: Accentuate the Positive, and Eliminate the Negative

Tip Five

Tell Your Story Well, Part A: Be Concise

By being "concise," I do not mean providing terse or incomplete answers to interview questions. Rather, I mean making sure that you fully answer the interviewer's questions with all of the relevant information he/she has requested—while avoiding long-winded answers full of extraneous information.

When you are not concise, an interviewer may tune you out or become bored with the conversation; if you are verbose, you can bury an interviewer in so much extraneous information that he/she may miss your key points. Finally, how crisply and well you tell your story—particularly at the outset—is critical for making a positive first impression. For this reason, it is important that you provide just the right amount of information when answering interview questions.

EXAMPLE 5–1

Let's use an example to better illustrate this advice. In this example, a candidate is applying for an entry-level position in a law firm. Using a BEI-type question, let's examine the candidate's answer and the story he/she tells. I will break this answer into each part of the story—situation, behavior, and results—in order to highlight how this and subsequent advice can affect how well or how poorly candidates tell a story. Let's start with the *situation*.

INTERVIEWER'S QUESTION

Tell me about a time when you were faced with conflicting priorities. (**Situation**)

How did you determine your top priority? (Behavior)

And what happened as a result? (Results)

CANDIDATE'S ANSWER

(Situation) *Once when I was doing a summer internship in another law firm, I was given three different assignments by three different partners in the firm. Two of the partners who gave me assignments were not my boss, and one was my boss. These three partners didn't know one another well, and none of them knew what assignments the others had given me. All three assignments were due within the same week. I remember that week well. It was July, and it was the hottest July on record. I pay attention to that, because my birthday is in July, and I always notice how hot it is around my birthday. Anyway, I knew quality would suffer if I tried to do each assignment at the same time. The first assignment was to do some research about the precedents in a particular case. The case was an interesting one and had even been in the local newspapers a while back. The second assignment was to make a few calls to the local courts to find out the schedule of trials for our law firm over the next few months. The court clerks usually have that schedule a few months in advance. Some of them are more on top of the schedules than others, but most of them should have access to the calendar. The third assignment was to write a brief for one of the senior attorneys about one of his cases that had to do with a lawsuit that had been filed against a major company in the area. The case was about a company that terminated a number of its employees without advance warning, and the employees banded together to file a class action lawsuit for wrongful termination.*

Are you tired of listening to that candidate's story yet? I know I am, and I'm sure the interviewer is, too. That's because the candidate did not heed the tip to *be concise.*

It is easy, and sometimes deadly, to provide too much unimportant detail, especially when describing a situation. Not only will your interviewer be turned off but many of the details may be completely irrelevant to your answer.

Remember what interviewers really want to know by asking you BEI-type questions. They do not particularly care about the situation itself, and they certainly don't care about superfluous information, such as how July can be. Instead, they want to learn just enough about the situation to allow them to understand your behavior and results—so that they can then deduce your character, competence, and chemistry/compatibility. Take care only to provide enough of a description of the situation to allow the interviewer to understand the context of your actions—and no more. If your interviewer wants more detail about the situation, he/she will ask you for it.

Now let's revise the "situation" portion of the candidate's answer, this time removing the extraneous information and heeding the caution to be concise.

CANDIDATE'S ANSWER—REVISED
(Situation) *When I was doing a summer internship in another law firm, I was given three different assignments by three different partners in the firm, one of whom was my boss. None of those partners knew that the others had also given me assignments. All three assignments were due within the same week, and it was not possible to complete each in a high-quality manner within the same time frame.*

That is a sufficient description of the situation. It includes the relevant information and no more. The interviewer doesn't need to know (and doesn't care about) details about the weather, the assignments, or how court clerks behave. This description is just enough to appropriately set the stage for the candidate to describe his/her behavior and results. Again, if the interviewer wants to know more about the situation, he/she can probe further.

NOW YOU TRY IT!
Now that you have the basic idea of being concise, try answering the "situation" portion of the same BEI interview question, based on a situation from

your own experience. Concentrate on including only relevant information and providing just enough context so that the interviewer has a good understanding of what you faced. Be careful not to include needless detail that will make the interviewer tune you out or miss your key points. Remember, for this practice exercise, just answer the "situation" part of the question.

INTERVIEWER'S QUESTION
Tell me about a time when you were faced with conflicting priorities. **(Situation)**

How did you determine your top priority? (Behavior)

And what happened as a result? (Results)

YOUR ANSWER: (SITUATION)

_____
_____
_____
_____

WHAT DO YOU THINK?
How do you think you did? Did you convey the situation in a complete but concise manner? Did you provide the interviewer with enough of a description to understand the situation you were facing without going into too much unnecessary detail? Did the interviewer have sufficient context to understand your behavior and results?

_____
_____
_____
_____

SUMMARY: TIP 5
Answering interview questions often requires that you tell stories about yourself; these stories paint a portrait of who you are (your character, competence,

and chemistry/compatibility) for the interviewer. When telling your story, you need to make sure not only to answer your interviewer's questions fully but also to heed a few tips that are essential to telling your story well.

One of these tips is to *be concise*. Particularly when describing the situation, be careful to answer the interviewer's question completely, but avoid providing long-winded answers that include extraneous information. Provide the interviewer with just enough information to understand the context of your behavior and results. Heeding this caution will keep the interviewer from tuning you out and having to dig through a mountain of irrelevant information when trying to determine if you are a good match for the position.

Tell Your Story Well, Part B: Highlight Key Messages

Highlighting key messages means that while you are telling your story during the interview, you purposely emphasize what you think the interviewer is looking for most.

Tip 4 is related to this tip, because doing your homework beforehand and having a good understanding of the qualifications the interviewer is looking for (from studying the position description) both help you to know which key messages to highlight when you answer interview questions.

Tip 5 is also related to this tip, because being verbose can prevent the interviewer from seeing the match between your qualifications and the position requirements. In addition to the boredom factor, the worst thing about information overload is that your listeners may become so buried by extraneous information that they may have to dig to find what they are looking for in your story, and therefore they might miss the "forest" for the "trees."

Tip 6 goes even further than these two tips. Even if they do not add extraneous information, sometimes people do not make those significant nuggets explicit enough for the interviewer to clearly see how well they match the position requirements. This tip means intentionally highlighting the key messages in your answers so that interviewers can easily recognize the match.

As you now know, by carefully listening to your answers to their questions, interviewers try to determine the degree to which your character, competence, and chemistry/compatibility match their needs. Because of this, it is important that you help the interviewer clearly see how your background and experience match the desired qualifications by explicitly highlighting those key messages in your answers.

To understand this better, let's use the same BEI-type question we used when discussing Tip 5.

INTERVIEWER'S QUESTION

Tell me about a time when you were faced with conflicting priorities. (Situation)

How did you determine your top priority? (Behavior)

And what happened as a result? (Results)

As a refresher, here is the concise way in which the candidate described the situation in Tip 5:

> (Situation) *When I was doing a summer internship in another law firm, I was given three different assignments by three different partners in the firm, one of whom was my boss. None of those partners knew that the others had also given me assignments. All three assignments were due within the same week, and it was not possible to complete each in a high-quality manner within the same time frame.*

EXAMPLE 6–1

Now, keeping both tips 5 and 6 in mind, let's focus on the "behavior" part of this same question in order to explore how you can keep your answers concise while still highlighting the key messages in your story.

INTERVIEWER'S QUESTION

Tell me about a time when you were faced with conflicting priorities. (Situation)

How did you determine your top priority? **(Behavior)**

And what happened as a result? (Results)

CANDIDATE'S ANSWER

(Behavior) *The first thing I did was to do a little digging on both the importance of each assignment and the flexibility of the deadlines. Like I mentioned, the first assignment was to do some research about the precedents in a particular case. I found out that another intern was also working on that case. As it turns out, that person went to my law school and was a friend of a friend. He told me that he had already found some good precedents and that the case would probably not go to trial for six months—if it ended up being tried at all.*

My second assignment was given to me by my boss; this was the one about making a few calls to the local courts to find out the schedule of trials for our law firm over the next few months. At one of the firm's staff meetings, I learned that the lawyers in the firm all needed that schedule yesterday and that it was critical to update the firm's calendar, which was out of date and had already been the cause of three late or missed court appearances by the firm. That was really embarrassing for the firm, and one of those missed appearances actually resulted in the firm receiving a fine.

The third assignment was to write a brief for one of the senior attorneys about one of his cases that had to do with a lawsuit that was filed against a major company in the area. As you may recall, that case was about a company that terminated a number of its employees without advance warning, and the employees banded together to file a class action lawsuit for wrongful termination. When digging around for information about that one, I found out that the senior attorney was someone who really liked to be ahead of the game and that this case, while important, had been put on hold for a while. Nevertheless, the senior attorney

39

wanted to get the brief done now anyway. I then took the conflicting priorities to my boss, shared my findings with him, and suggested a proposed sequence and timing for completing the assignments.

Asleep yet? Almost feel sorry for the interviewer? Yes, you guessed it; too much information—again. And the interviewers may miss the most important key messages the candidate wants them to hear about his/her behavior in the situation—not only because the messages were buried but because they were not made explicit.

In order to make the key messages about your behavior in a situation explicit, you must first reflect on what your key messages really are and then how to say them in a way that is both concise and clear.

But how do you know what key messages to highlight? The *position description* is your best tool in that regard. You should study it thoroughly in advance to fully understand the company's needs and how your background and qualifications would meet those needs.

In this instance, let's suppose the position description included "character" words such as *independent* and *problem solver* and "competence" words such as *research skills*. Given that information, let's revise the "behavior" portion of the candidate's answer, this time removing the extraneous information and highlighting the key messages (by heeding the advice of both tips 5 and 6).

CANDIDATE'S ANSWER—REVISED

(Behavior) *The first thing I did was to conduct some **independent research** on each assignment, including ascertaining their importance and the flexibility of their deadlines. I learned that the first assignment would probably not go to trial for at least six months, if it ended up being tried at all. I discovered that the second assignment was highly time sensitive and had high visibility and importance for the whole firm. The third assignment was in support of a case that had recently been put on hold for an indefinite period of time. After completing my **research**, I took the three conflicting priorities to my boss, and I shared my findings with him. I offered him a proposed **solution to the problem**, including a suggested sequence for completing the assignments based on importance and the flexibility of the timing.*

Do you see the differences between the original and revised answers about the behavior that the candidate has described? The first answer was so cumbersome and lengthy that the interviewer might have tuned the person out, thus missing the key messages. And although the key messages did appear somewhere in the original answer, they were not as explicitly stated as in the revised answer.

The position description said the company was looking for someone who was "independent" and had good "research skills." Both the original and revised candidate answers included references to those, but in the revised answer, they were more clearly called out. For example, in the first sentence of the original answer, the candidate talks about doing a "little digging." In the revised answer, the candidate talks about doing some "independent research," thus delivering two key messages in one.

The final sentence in the revised answer directly hits the word "research" again; the job description also calls for someone who is a "problem solver." While both the original and revised answers discuss the approach the candidate took to solving the problem, the final sentence of the original answer talks about taking the "proposed sequence" to the candidate's manager, whereas the revised answer overtly highlights taking the proposed *solution to the problem* to the candidate's manager.

Why take a chance that the interviewer might not make the connection between what he/she is looking for and what you have to offer? If you were the car salesperson in Tip 3, and you knew that the buyer was looking for a vehicle with all-wheel drive and a navigation system, why would you not clearly state that? You should not take a chance that the buyer might miss your point by either not mentioning it at all or saying it in an unclear way (for example, by saying the car has "tools to help with directions" rather than saying the car has a "navigation system"). Remember, you are the "seller" in an interviewer situation, so both knowing what the "buyer" is looking for (via the position description) and then clearly highlighting those messages in your answer are critical.

EXAMPLE 6–2

Now, let's conclude with the "results" portion of the candidate's answer, again keeping in mind the advice from Tip 5 (be concise) and Tip 6 (highlight key messages).

INTERVIEWER'S QUESTION

Tell me about a time when you were faced with conflicting priorities. (Situation)

How did you determine your top priority? (Behavior)

And what happened as a result? **(Results)**

CANDIDATE'S ANSWER

(Results) *My boss was interested in what I had done, and he asked me to review my findings about each of the priorities with him. We spent some time talking about each of the priorities, and he told me a story about a time when he had conflicting priorities and how frustrating that was for him. He had more questions about the first case than the others, so I offered to get even more information for him. I made an appointment with the person who was handling the first case, and I got some additional information. Then I set up a second meeting with my boss, and I shared the additional information with him. After reviewing everything, my boss accepted my proposed sequencing; he thanked me for coming to him with a proposed approach versus coming to him with only a problem and leaving it to him to figure it out. Then he wrote a note to the people in charge of the other priorities and told them about the revised timeline and his rationale for the changes. He asked them to let him know if they had any concerns, but none of them did. In the end, all three of the priorities were completed, but over the course of a month instead of all in the same week.*

Again, there is too much extraneous information and not enough emphasis on important words, which clouds the candidate's key messages. Let's review a revised answer that uses the advice given in tips 5 and 6.

CANDIDATE'S ANSWER—REVISED

(Results) *My boss and I reviewed my **research** findings, and he accepted my proposal. He thanked me for coming to him with a **well-researched solution** versus coming to him with a problem. He negotiated the revised deadlines with the other two requestors, and I completed all of the priorities according to the new timeline. There were no adverse impacts to the clients or to the firm, and everyone was pleased with the quality of the work that had been done on each project.*

INSIDE THE MIND OF THE INTERVIEWER

Now let's put all three revised pieces of the candidate's answer (situation, behavior, and results) together; we'll go inside the mind of the interviewer to see what character, competence, and chemistry/compatibility perceptions the interviewer gained, based on the candidate's story.

Interviewer's Question: *Tell me about a time when you were faced with conflicting priorities. How did you determine the top priority? And what happened as a result?*

Candidate's Answer:

When I was doing a summer internship in another law firm, I was given three different assignments by three different partners in the firm, one of whom was my boss. None of those partners knew that the others had also given me assignments. All three assignments were due within the same week, and it was not possible to complete each in a high-quality manner within the same time frame.

The first thing I did was to conduct some independent research on each assignment, including ascertaining their importance and the flexibility of their deadlines. I learned that the first assignment would probably not go to trial for at least six months, if it ended up being tried at all. I discovered that the second assignment was highly time sensitive and had high visibility and importance for the whole firm. The third assignment was in support of a case that had recently been put on hold for an indefinite period of time. After completing my research, I took the three conflicting priorities to my boss, and I shared my findings with him. I offered him a proposed solution to the problem, including a suggested sequence for completing the assignments based on importance and the flexibility of the timing.

My boss and I reviewed my research findings, and he accepted my proposal. He thanked me for coming to him with a well-researched solution versus coming to him with a problem. He negotiated the revised deadlines with the other two requestors, and I completed all of the priorities according to the new timeline. There were no adverse impacts to the clients or to the firm, and everyone was pleased with the quality of the work that had been done on each project.

Interviewer's Thoughts		
Character	**Competence**	**Chemistry/Compatibility**
This candidate seems to be proactive and have the ability to think and work independently, which is exactly what we are looking for. This candidate not only seems to have the attributes we are seeking, but he/she also cares about the impact of his/her decisions on the firm and its clients.	This candidate has had relevant law-firm experience. This candidate has demonstrated research skills, which is another thing we are looking for. This candidate seems to have good judgment and critical-thinking skills. This candidate seems to be good at problem-solving, which is a key skill for this position.	It would be great to work with this kind of person, who doesn't just complain or get burdened by problems, but who independently goes about solving them and bringing forward solutions that keep the good of the firm and its clients in mind. He/she would set a good example for others.

WHAT DO YOU THINK?

What do you think of the candidate's entire answer? Do you see how the candidate heeds the advice that was given not only in tips 5 and 6 but also in tips 1–6? How do you think being concise and highlighting key messages makes it easier for the interviewer to gain a clear understanding of how well the candidate matches the position requirements and for the interviewer to gain a positive impression of the candidate's 3 Cs?

Important note: When possible, try to highlight key messages right at the beginning of your answer. This is because *people tend to remember what you say first*. For example, let's say that you are applying for a teaching position and the position description described the need to use data in student assessments. If you were asked a question about how you have evaluated students in the past, you might open your answer with something like, "I believe that the use of data is critical when assessing student performance." Then you could go on to describe a related situation, behavior and results and point out how you used data in that instance. By doing this, you are highlighting your key message right up front (where it will be remembered best) as well as within your story.

_____

_____

_____

_____

NOW YOU TRY IT!

Now that you've got the idea of tips 5 and 6, try answering the "situation," "behavior," and "results" portions of the same BEI-type interview question based on a situation from your own experience. You can use either the same situation you described in Tip 5's "Now You Try It!" section or a different situation.

Remember to be concise and to highlight key messages. To help you highlight key messages, first think about what knowledge, skills, and character traits the interviewer is looking for. (If you have a position description to use, that would be helpful here; if not, think about what the interviewer might be looking for when filling a position that you might apply for.) Jot down on the lines below four things that you believe an interviewer might be looking for in your response, and then try your hand at highlighting those key messages in your answer.

_____ , _____ , _____ , _____

INTERVIEWER'S QUESTION

Tell me about a time when you were faced with conflicting priorities. (Situation)

How did you determine your top priority? (Behavior)

And what happened as a result? (Results)

YOUR ANSWER
(Situation)

_____
_____
_____
_____

(Behavior)

_____
_____
_____
_____

(Results)

_____
_____
_____
_____

INSIDE THE MIND OF THE INTERVIEWER
Now try putting yourself inside the mind of the interviewer. Copy your answer into the table below. Based on your answer, populate the rest of the table with what you think the interviewer's thoughts might be about your character, competence, and chemistry/compatibility. Include how well you believe the interviewer will think your qualifications will match what he/she is looking for (the qualifications you wrote down on the lines above your answer).

Interviewer's Question: *Tell me about a time when you were faced with conflicting priorities. How did you determine the top priority? And what happened as a result?*

Your Answer:

Interviewer's Thoughts		
Character	Competence	Chemistry/Compatibility

WHAT DO YOU THINK?

Do you think you impressed the interviewer with your answer? Why do you think this? How well do you think your answer presented your character, competence, and chemistry/compatibility? Given the requirements you felt the interviewer was looking for (i.e., what you wrote on the four lines above your answer), how explicitly or clearly did you highlight them in your answer? How much of a match do you think the interviewer found between your answer and the position requirements?

_____

_____

_____

_____

SUMMARY: TIP 6

Answering interview questions often requires that you tell stories about yourself; these stories paint a portrait of who you are (your character, competence, and chemistry/compatibility) for the interviewer. When telling your story, you need to make sure not only to answer your interviewer's questions fully but also to heed a few tips that are essential to telling your story well.

One tip is to highlight key messages. This means helping the interviewer see how well you match the position requirements by clearly emphasizing these requirements in your answers. Doing your homework beforehand and having a good understanding of what qualifications the interviewer is looking for will help you to be aware of what key messages to highlight when you answer interview questions. Your best source for that information is the position description.

Tell Your Story Well, Part C: Accentuate the Positive, and Eliminate the Negative

"You've got to accentuate the positive, eliminate the negative" is the first line of an old song that was popular long before your time (and even mine). You may be more familiar with the adage, "If you can't say something nice, don't say anything at all." The spirit of both of these sayings is also relevant for interviews.

Saying positive things during an interview involves making favorable comments and expressing gratitude when you talk about previous employers, coworkers, and work experiences. That means focusing on the benefits and opportunities you gained and the lessons you learned from prior jobs, projects, bosses, and companies.

Saying negative things during an interview means speaking unfavorably about your present or past employers and coworkers, your work history and experiences, and even about yourself. Saying negative things can only hurt you during the interview process. Remember, as you learned from Tip 2, the best predictor of your future performance is your past performance. Interviewers realize that if you say negative things about others you have worked with (or for) in the past, you are equally likely to speak negatively about them (your new employer, coworkers, and job) in the future.

Because some interview questions may be phrased in such a way that they entice you to speak negatively about yourself or others, it is important to know how to answer them in a way that accentuates the positive and does not reflect poorly on you during the interview process.

EXAMPLE 7–1

Let's use a couple of examples to illustrate this point. In the first example, we will use a typical interview question that is phrased in such a way that you may be tempted to say something negative, particularly if you are unhappy with your current employer. In this scenario, let's suppose there are two candidates (A and B) who work as medical researchers at the same small research lab. Both are equally unhappy with their current jobs and are interviewing for a position at a larger national lab called Major Medical Research Labs.

Let's look at the answers from Candidate A and Candidate B to this typical interview question.

INTERVIEWER'S QUESTION
Why do you want to leave your current job?

ANSWER: CANDIDATE A
My current employer is terrible. My hours are long, and because the team is small, I have to do a lot of the research myself. My coworkers are unfriendly, and I have a horrible boss. I am seeking a better position with better hours and better people in a bigger lab.

ANSWER: CANDIDATE B
I have worked for my current employer for the past five years. Because it is a small lab, I have had the opportunity to work on many projects and hone my research skills. I have always admired the broader mission, scope, and impact of Major Medical Research Labs, and I would consider it a privilege to leverage my skills and experience to make an even wider contribution to this field of research.

INSIDE THE MIND OF THE INTERVIEWER
Now let's go back inside the mind of the interviewer again to see how the candidates' answers in the example above might influence the interviewer's thoughts about the candidates' 3 Cs and how their positive and negative comments may affect the interviewer's thoughts.

Interviewer's Question: *Why do you want to leave your current job?*

Answer: Candidate A

My current employer is terrible. My hours are long, and I have to do a lot of the research myself, because the team is small. My coworkers are unfriendly, and I have a horrible boss. I am seeking a better position with better hours and better people in a bigger lab.

Interviewer's Thoughts

Character	Competence	Chemistry/Compatibility
This candidate seems critical and judgmental. If he/she is that way about his/her current employer, he/she will likely be that way about us.	This candidate seems to possess the research skills and experience we require.	I wonder how this candidate would get along with others here, since he/she doesn't get along with either his/her peers or superiors now.
I wonder about this candidate's work ethic. He/she is complaining about the hours.		We certainly don't need a negative influence or disgruntled employee on our team.
Every reason this candidate is giving about leaving his/her current employer is self-serving. I wonder if he/she is concerned with anyone other than him/herself.		

Interviewer's Question: *Why do you want to leave your current job?*

Answer: Candidate B

I have worked for my current employer for the past five years. As it is a small lab, I have had the opportunity to work on many projects and hone my research skills. I have always admired the broader mission, scope, and impact of Major Medical Research Labs, and I would consider it a privilege to leverage my skills and experience to make an even wider contribution to this field of research.

Interviewer's Thoughts

Character	Competence	Chemistry/Compatibility
This candidate seems appreciative, grateful, humble, and upbeat.	This candidate seems to possess the research skills and experience we require.	A person with this type of attitude and desire to serve would be a positive influence on our team.
This candidate seems genuinely interested in making a contribution to the field, not just bettering his/her own circumstance.	This candidate is knowledgeable about our mission and scope.	

WHAT DO YOU THINK?

Let's say you are Candidate A. What do you think of your answer? How did saying negative things affect the interviewer's perceptions of you? Also, as we discussed in Tip 3, *who* do you think your answer is about? Yes—it's about *you*. Your answer is about what the position could do for *you*.

In contrast, let's say you are Candidate B. What do you think of your answer? How did focusing on the positive aspects of your current position, and expressing gratitude about your previous experience, affect the interviewer's perceptions of you? And *who* do you think your answer is about? It's about *them* and doing something for *them*.

Based on these answers, which candidate do you think is more likely to get the job? Candidate B, of course. And who do you think most influenced that decision? *You* did.

These answers provide another example of how character can trump competence in an interview, especially when competence is fairly equal among candidates. In this situation, both candidates seem to have the medical research skills and experience required for the position. And yet, if you are Candidate B, you have the advantage, primarily because of what your answer indicates about your character (as well as your chemistry/compatibility).

NOW YOU TRY IT!

Now that you've got the idea, try to answer the following typical interview question in a way that accents the positive and doesn't hint of anything negative. Based on your own work history, think of a time you wanted to leave a job because you were unhappy there. Imagine that you are applying for a new position in order to leave the job you were or are dissatisfied with.

INTERVIEWER'S QUESTION
Why do you want to leave your job?

YOUR ANSWER

_____

_____

_____

_____

INSIDE THE MIND OF THE INTERVIEWER
Now try putting yourself inside the mind of the interviewer. Copy your answer into the table below. Then, based on your answer, jot down what you think the interviewer's thoughts might be about your character, competence, and chemistry/compatibility, particularly given your attitude toward your current employer.

Interviewer's Question: *Why do you want to leave your job?*		
Your Answer:		
Interviewer's Thoughts		
Character	Competence	Chemistry/Compatibility

WHAT DO YOU THINK?

Given your answer, and how positively or negatively you spoke about the employer you are dissatisfied with, how do you think you influenced the interviewer's perception of you? Why do you think so?

_____

_____

_____

_____

THINGS THAT HAVE GONE WRONG

Other types of interview questions whose phrasing can tempt you to speak negatively are those that relate to things that have gone wrong in your career or work history. Interviewers will often probe you about those situations, and they will ask you to describe what went wrong. You may wonder how you can answer these types of questions in a positive yet honest way. In my experience, the best way is to heed the saying that "A mistake is not a failure if you learn from it."

The best way to make something positive out of something negative is to admit the error and then describe the positive things you learned from the experience. This also shows the interviewer that you have the humility and maturity to accept personal responsibility for your mistakes (and not blame others for them). The interviewer will see this as a positive character trait, because it shows you are humble and open enough to be a good learner.

EXAMPLE 7–2

To illustrate this point, let's use another typical interview question and consider two potential answers. In this scenario, there are two candidates (A and B) who work as software engineers at the same technical company. Both were involved in the same software development project that went wrong a few years back.

INTERVIEWER'S QUESTION

Tell me about a time when you were involved in a project that failed.

Important note: The question above is a good example of a BEI-type question that does *not* clearly call out the "situation, behavior, and results" structure. When this happens, remember that it is still important to include all three parts of the story (situation, behavior, and results) in your answer.

ANSWER: CANDIDATE A

I was part of a global project team that was responsible for the coding and installation of a new software system for an important client. It was an ambitious project that was on a tight time line. And it was complicated, because many people were involved, and each team member was in a different country and in a different time zone. This meant that it was difficult to communicate with one another. As a result, the project didn't come in on time.

One beneficial result of this failure, though, was that it taught me several valuable lessons. I used to think that having a good project plan with deliverables and milestones was the primary key to project success. I learned from this experience that a good communication plan is also critical and that it is especially important when the key players are geographically dispersed. Now, if my boss doesn't already have one in place, I volunteer to create a communication plan for each project I am involved in, and I've taught others to do the same. This practice has helped increase our firm's customer satisfaction and our project success rate.

ANSWER: CANDIDATE B

I was part of a global project team that was responsible for the coding and installation of a new software system for an important client. It was an ambitious project that was on a tight time line. And it was complicated, because many people were involved, and each team member was in a different country and in a different time zone. This meant that it was difficult to communicate with one another.

My boss didn't do anything about the communication issues, and I became frustrated with him as time went on. The project didn't come in on time or on budget. The client was disappointed, and I looked bad to them, even though I had done my part on the project. As a result, I vowed to never work on a dispersed global team again.

INSIDE THE MIND OF THE INTERVIEWER

Now let's go back inside the mind of the interviewer again to see how the candidates' answers in the example above might influence the interviewer's thoughts about the candidates' 3 Cs and how the negative and positive comments may affect the interviewer's thoughts.

Interviewer's Question: *Tell me about a time when you were involved in a project that failed.*		
Answer: Candidate A		
I was part of a global project team that was responsible for the coding and installation of a new software system for an important client. It was an ambitious project that was on a tight timeline. And it was complicated, because many people were involved, and each team member was in a different country and in a different time zone. This meant that it was difficult to communicate with one another. As a result, the project didn't come in on time. *One beneficial result of this failure, though, was that it taught me several valuable lessons. I used to think that having a good project plan with deliverables and milestones was the primary key to project success. I learned from this experience that a good communication plan is also critical and that it is especially important when the key players are geographically dispersed. Now, if my boss doesn't already have one in place, I volunteer to create a communication plan for each project I am involved in, and I've taught others to do the same. This practice has helped increase our firm's customer satisfaction and our project success rate.*		
Interviewer's Thoughts		
Character	**Competence**	**Chemistry/Compatibility**
This candidate seems honest enough to share a real example of a project that didn't go well and didn't meet its deadline. This candidate seems humble and mature enough to learn from this experience. This candidate seems to be a self-starter, team player, and supportive employee. This candidate seems to have a service orientation, a willingness to share knowledge, and a desire to help others learn and grow.	This candidate seems to possess knowledge of the key requirements of a successful project, including a solid project plan (with all its component parts) and a good communication plan. This candidate has strong enough communication planning knowledge and skills to teach others how to do it.	This candidate's attributes and demonstrated desire to serve would make him/her a likeable and positive addition to our team.

Interviewer's Question: *Tell me about a time when you were involved in a project that failed.*

Answer: Candidate B

I was part of a global project team that was responsible for the coding and installation of a new software system for an important client. It was an ambitious project that was on a tight time line. And it was complicated, because many people were involved, and each team member was in a different country and in a different time zone. This meant that it was difficult to communicate with one another.

My boss didn't do anything about the communication issues, and I became frustrated with him as time went on. The project didn't come in on time or on budget. The client was disappointed, and I looked bad to them, even though I had done my part on the project. As a result, I vowed to never work on a dispersed global team again.

Interviewer's Thoughts		
Character	**Competence**	**Chemistry/Compatibility**
This candidate seems honest enough to share a real example of a project that didn't go well and didn't meet its deadline. This candidate seems to be the kind of person who blames others for mistakes and who does not take personal accountability, ownership, or responsibility for problems. This candidate seems self-focused and more worried about impacts to him/herself than about impacts to others. This candidate doesn't seem to be much of a team player or to learn much from his/her mistakes.	This candidate does not seem to have acquired knowledge or skill in how to create and implement a project communication plan.	I'm not sure I want our employees to work alongside or be negatively influenced by the type of person who blames others, points upward, only worries about him/herself, and doesn't learn from mistakes.

WHAT DO YOU THINK?

Let's say you are Candidate A. What do you think of your answer? How did admitting the issue and then discussing the positive lessons that you learned affect the interviewer's perceptions of you? And how did focusing on the positive lead the interviewer to perceive your character traits?

Now let's say you are Candidate B. What do you think of your answer? How did focusing on the negative affect the interviewer's perceptions of you? What do you think of the supposed "lesson learned" you expressed in your answer? And *who* do you think your answer is about? Again, as warned about in Tip 3, this answer focuses on *you*—and the impact on *you*. How did that (and the rest of your answer) affect the interviewer's perceptions of your character?

Based on these answers, which candidate do you think is more likely to get the job? Candidate A, of course. And, again, who do you think most influenced that decision? *You* did.

NOW YOU TRY IT!

Now that you've got the idea, try answering the BEI-type interview question we used in Example 7–2 in a way that accentuates the positive and doesn't hint of anything negative. Think of a project that you were involved in that didn't go well, and try to answer the question in a way that highlights not only the project's issues but the positive lessons that you learned from the experience. Remember to include all three parts of the story (situation, behavior, and results) in your answer.

INTERVIEWER'S QUESTION

Tell me about a time when you were involved in a project that failed.

YOUR ANSWER

(Situation)

_____

_____

_____

(Behavior)

_____

_____

_____

(Results)

_____

_____

_____

INSIDE THE MIND OF THE INTERVIEWER

Now put yourself inside the mind of the interviewer. Based on your answer, jot down what you think the interviewer's thoughts might be about your character, competence, and chemistry/compatibility, particularly given how positive or negative your response was about a challenging situation.

Interviewer's Question: *Tell me about a time when you were involved in a project that failed.*		
Your Answer:		
Interviewer's Thoughts		
Character	**Competence**	**Chemistry/Compatibility**

WHAT DO YOU THINK?

Based on your answer, how do you think you did? Why do you think so? How do you think your positive or negative comments influenced the interviewer's thoughts about you as a candidate?

_____

_____

_____

_____

NEGATIVE STORY ENDINGS

Another strategy to keep in mind is to try to use examples and tell stories that have happy endings—those that end on a positive note instead of a negative one. For example, during an interview, suppose your interviewer asks, "Tell me about a time when you demonstrated courage." Let's say two possible stories from your past experience immediately come to mind. One was when you demonstrated courage by standing up for a fellow employee when the management team wanted to fire him, but management didn't listen to you and fired the employee anyway. The other example you think of was when you demonstrated courage by advocating for a politically unpopular decision that you felt would be the right decision for your company. The management did listen to you that time, and the decision yielded a great deal of success for the organization.

Which of those two examples do you think you should select when telling a story about courage—the one with the positive outcome or the one with the negative outcome? It is better, whenever possible, to use examples with positive results. Just as first impressions are important when you begin your story, final impressions are also important and memorable. It is better for your story endings to be positive rather than negative.

SPEAKING NEGATIVELY ABOUT YOURSELF

Finally, try not to say anything negative about yourself. Again, your interviewer will tempt you with questions like, "What are your greatest strengths and weaknesses?" When an interviewer asks that you share your weaknesses, remember that you are painting a portrait of yourself and that you need to be careful not to tarnish that image.

When I am asked that kind of question, if possible I like to couple the answer about strengths and weaknesses so that they will offset each other. For example, I might say something like, "One of my greatest strengths is my attention to detail. But I find that when I overuse that strength, it can actually become a weakness. If I focus too much on detail, I tend to put excessive effort into completing the task."

In that way, the weakness you share, although it may be true, is not too damaging to your self-portrait, and it is tied closely to your strength. Sometimes the interviewer may even welcome that kind of weakness: an employee who puts in tremendous effort may potentially be a valuable employee.

If you choose not to couple your strengths and weaknesses when answering this kind of question, try to share weaknesses that are expected, undamaging, and in the professional realm, rather than ones that are surprising, worrisome, and/or more personal in nature. For example, if you are applying for a college internship and you do not yet have any relevant work experience, you can offer the weakness of "inexperience," since that is true, expected, and harmless in that situation. This is preferable to offering something like "procrastination," which would not be expected or welcomed and could create concern about your character.

SUMMARY: TIP 7

Answering interview questions often requires that you tell stories about yourself; these stories paint a portrait of who you are (your character, competence, and chemistry/compatibility) for the interviewer. When telling your story, you need to make sure not only to answer your interviewer's questions fully but also to heed a few tips that are essential to telling your story well.

One of these tips is to speak positively and avoid speaking negatively during your interview. Speaking positively means making favorable comments and expressing gratitude when talking about previous employers, bosses, coworkers, and work experiences. This involves focusing on the benefits, opportunities, and lessons that you have learned from them.

Speaking negatively means speaking unfavorably about your present or past employers, bosses, coworkers, or work experiences and even about yourself. Saying negative things can only hurt you during the interview process.

Because some interview questions may be phrased in such a way that they actually entice you to speak negatively about yourself or others, it is important to know how to answer these questions in a way that will accentuate the positive and will not reflect negatively on you during the interview process.

Tip Eight

Tell Your Story Well, Part D: Mind Your Attitude

By "minding your attitude," I am referring to paying attention to your demeanor during the interview process. This includes not only your words but also your tone and your manner in such things as your enthusiasm, energy, arrogance, humility, confidence, meekness, belligerence, superiority, inferiority, respectfulness, disrespectfulness, and so on. This often involves finding an attitude "sweet spot." By this, I mean a middle ground that is well balanced between two attitudinal extremes; for example, the sweet spot between superiority and inferiority is confidence.

Most of us have been reprimanded at one time or another with the words "It's not just what you said; it's how you said it." The same is true during interviews. Because both the words you speak and the manner in which you speak them are important in forming the interviewer's perceptions of you, it is important to pay attention to your attitude and to find the attitude "sweet spot" as you conduct yourself and tell your story.

EXAMPLE 8–1

Since our first example focuses not on *what* is said but rather on *how* it is said—the attitude you convey by your unspoken demeanor—we will not use our typical format for the following example.

Suppose you are applying for a cruise director position on a ship. The position involves welcoming passengers; ensuring they are having fun; and keeping them engaged, excited, and interested in cruise activities. Let's say you meet the basic requirements of the job description in terms of your education and experience, but during the interview you are expressionless, lethargic, slouched back in your seat, and fairly passive in your attitude. What would the interviewer think about your match for the position, even if you are qualified in terms of competence and experience?

Alternatively, suppose that while you are being interviewed for this position, you are smiling, bright-eyed, and outgoing, and you show enthusiasm, energy and excitement as you discuss the role and your qualifications for it. What would the interviewer think about your match for the position? Clearly, the interviewer will be more inclined to hire you if your unspoken demeanor fits the latter description, since both your attitude and your words during the interview process help convey how well you match the position requirements.

Important note: Even when the job requirements do not call for enthusiasm as clearly as a cruise director position would, it is always important to demonstrate sincere enthusiasm and a high energy level during your interview.

EXAMPLE 8–2

Now let's use our usual format to illustrate how attitude can also come across in the words you say during the interview process. For this example, we will consider the attitudes of superiority and inferiority—and the sweet spot between them, which we will call "confidence." In order to demonstrate this, we will use a scenario with three candidates—Candidates A, B, and C.

INTERVIEWER'S QUESTION
You are one of three finalists who are being considered for this position. Why are you the best candidate for this job?

ANSWER: CANDIDATE A
I am certain that I am better than any of the other candidates who are applying for this job. I have five years of experience, I am more intelligent than most people,

and I have exceptional skills. I tend to make every work environment better with my efforts and to outshine those I work with in anything I undertake.

ANSWER: CANDIDATE B

I doubt that I am better than any of the other candidates. With my five years of experience, I hope that I am at least as good as some of them. I know I would be lucky to get this job, and I will try my best not to let you down.

ANSWER: CANDIDATE C

When I read the job description, I was struck by the degree of match between my qualifications and the position requirements. I have five years of experience and a passion for this work. I have always admired this company and would consider it a privilege to contribute to its success.

INSIDE THE MIND OF THE INTERVIEWER

Now let's go inside the mind of the interviewer to see how each of the candidates' answers in the example above might influence his/her thoughts about the candidates' 3 Cs and which of the candidates hit the desired "sweet spot."

Interviewer's Question: *You are one of three finalists who are being considered for this position. Why are you the best candidate for this job?*		
Answer: Candidate A		
I am certain that I am better than any of the other candidates who are applying for this job. I have five years of experience, I am more intelligent than most people, and I have exceptional skills. I tend to make every work environment better with my efforts and to outshine those I work with in anything I undertake.		
Interviewer's Thoughts		
Character	**Competence**	**Chemistry/Compatibility**
This candidate seems arrogant and narcissistic. He/she seems to have an extremely inflated opinion of him/herself.	This candidate has the experience we are seeking.	I wonder how this candidate would get along with others in our organization, since he/she seems to competitively compare him/herself with others and have an air of superiority. Would this candidate listen to and respect others' opinions and be able to build strong and productive working relationships?

Interviewer's Question: *You are one of three finalists who are being considered for this position. Why are you the best candidate for this job?*		
Answer: Candidate B		
I doubt that I am better than any of the other candidates. With my five years of experience, I hope that I am at least as good as some of them. I know I would be lucky to get this job, and I will try my best not to let you down.		
Interviewer's Thoughts		
Character	**Competence**	**Chemistry/Compatibility**
This candidate seems to have a good sense of self-worth and self-confidence as well as humility and a desire to serve.	This candidate has the experience we are seeking.	Would this candidate be strong enough to hold his/her own with the team and in the organization?
This candidate focused on summarizing his/her experience vs. comparing him/herself to others whom he/she does not even know.		Would this candidate be capable of standing up for him/herself, his team members, and his/her convictions when challenged?

Interviewer's Question: *You are one of three finalists who are being considered for this position. Why are you the best candidate for this job?*		
Answer: Candidate C		
When I read the job description, I was struck by the degree of match between my qualifications and the position requirements. I have five years of experience and a passion for this work. I have always admired this company and would consider it a privilege to contribute to its success.		
Interviewer's Thoughts		
Character	**Competence**	**Chemistry/Compatibility**
This candidate seems to have a good sense of self-worth and self-confidence as well as humility and a desire to serve.	This candidate has the experience we are seeking.	This candidate seems to display the kind of demeanor, confidence, humility, and service orientation to allow him/her to get along well with others on the team.
This candidate focused on summarizing his/her experience vs. comparing him/herself to others whom he/she does not even know.		

WHAT DO YOU THINK?

Let's say you are Candidate A. What do you think of your answer? How did your words convey an attitude of superiority? And what did that attitude lead the interviewer to think about your character and chemistry/compatibility?

And let's say you are Candidate B. What do you think of your answer? How did your words convey an attitude of inferiority? And what did that attitude lead the interviewer to think about your character and chemistry/compatibility?

Finally, what if you are Candidate C? What do you think of your answer? Did you hit the attitude "sweet spot" between superiority and inferiority by displaying an aura of confidence without being overly arrogant or overly self-effacing?

Based on these answers, which candidate do you think would be most likely to get the job? Candidate C, of course. And do you see how attitude affected that hiring decision?

NOW YOU TRY IT!

Now that you understand the importance of minding your attitude during an interview, try to answer the following typical interview question in a way that hits the attitude sweet spot.

INTERVIEWER'S QUESTION

Why should we hire you for this job?

YOUR ANSWER

_____

_____

_____

_____

INSIDE THE MIND OF THE INTERVIEWER

Now try putting yourself inside the mind of the interviewer. Copy your answer into the table below. Considering your answer, jot down what you think the interviewer's thoughts might be about your character, competence, and chemistry/compatibility, particularly given the attitude that is conveyed by your answer.

Interviewer's Question: *Why should we hire you for this job?*		
Your Answer:		
Interviewer's Thoughts		
Character	Competence	Chemistry/Compatibility

WHAT DO YOU THINK?

Based on your answer and the thoughts you believe they evoked in the interviewer's mind, how well do you think you answered this question? To what extent did your attitude come through in your words? Did that attitude help or hurt you? Do you think you hit the attitude sweet spot?

_____

_____

_____

_____

SUMMARY: TIP 8

Answering interview questions often requires that you tell stories about yourself; these stories paint a portrait of who you are (your character, competence, and chemistry/compatibility) for the interviewer. When telling your story, you need to make sure not only to answer your interviewer's questions fully but also to heed a few tips that are essential to telling your story well.

One of these tips is to mind your *attitude*, which is conveyed by your words and demeanor during an interview. Your attitude includes such things as your enthusiasm, energy, arrogance, humility, confidence, meekness, belligerence, superiority, inferiority, respectfulness, disrespectfulness, and so on.

It is often good to find the attitude sweet spot when telling your story. That means projecting a balanced middle ground that is not too extreme in either direction; for example, the sweet spot between superiority and inferiority is confidence.

Tip Nine

Ask Good Questions — and Don't Ask Bad Ones

Toward the end of most interviews, interviewers usually ask if you have any questions you would like to ask them. You should always take advantage of that opportunity: be prepared to ask two or three good questions. This is important, but not necessarily for the reasons you may think. There are certain questions (which I call "bad questions") that you should *not* ask during an interview, no matter how much you want to know their answers. There are also questions that you may actually be less interested in learning the answers to that you *should* ask. I call these "good questions."

Good questions can help you appear intelligent and educated and like someone who has proactively done his/her homework beforehand. These questions can increase your attractiveness as a candidate. Bad questions, in contrast, can actually hurt your image and your candidacy. Understanding the difference between these two types of questions, and knowing how to prepare two or three good ones, will increase your chances of a successful interview.

BAD QUESTIONS

In Tip 3, as you'll recall, we discussed the fact that until you receive a written job offer, it's not about *you* (or what they can do for *you*); you are the seller, and at this point, you have no buying power. Bad questions include those that have to do with what *they* can do for *you* (vacations, benefits, promotions); bad questions also include those that imply that you have doubts, conditions, or worries about taking the job.

Even if you think you will not accept the job if the company does not offer a particular type of benefit, the interview is not the time to ask questions about benefits. Remember, once you have a written offer in hand, you and the interviewer change roles: you then become the buyer, and you now have buying power. At that point—and only at that point—should you ask questions about what *they* can do for *you* or about any concerns or conditions you may have.

It is also important to note that just because you receive a job offer, it doesn't mean you have to accept it. Your sole mission during the interview process should be to get the offer. Getting the offer does *not* commit you to taking the job: it simply gives you the option to consider it. After you receive the written offer, you can then ask any questions you may have about your needs or concerns. Then you can make your decision accordingly.

EXAMPLE 9–1

Let's look at an example of what *not* to ask. Let's say you are the candidate in this case.

INTERVIEWER'S QUESTION
Do you have any questions for me?

YOUR ANSWER
Could you tell me about your vacation policy and your paid company holidays?

INSIDE THE MIND OF THE INTERVIEWER
Now go inside the mind of the interviewer to see what your question may lead him/her to think about your 3 Cs.

Interviewer's Question: *Do you have any questions for me?*		
Your Answer: *Could you tell me about your vacation policy and your paid holidays?*		
Interviewer's Thoughts		
Character	**Competence**	**Chemistry/Compatibility**
Good grief. This candidate hasn't even started yet and is already thinking about time off. What kind of work ethic does this person have?	If that's the best question this candidate can come up with after our entire conversation, he/she must be a pretty shallow thinker.	I already have a couple of slackers in the ranks. I'd hate to add another one to the mix.

WHAT DO YOU THINK?

Given the interviewer's thoughts, what do you think about the quality of that question? Who is that question about? *You.* What is that question about? What they can do for *you.* What did that question make the interviewer think about your character, competence, and chemistry/compatibility? And who made the interviewer think that?

_____

_____

_____

_____

MORE EXAMPLES OF BAD QUESTIONS

You would probably get the same sort of negative reaction from the interviewer with questions like this:

- *Could you tell me about your policy on work-life balance?*
- *How frequently do you give pay raises?*
- *How soon will I be eligible for promotion?*
- *Do you give bonuses?*

Again, even if you are very interested in the answers to some or all of these types of questions, and even if your decision to take the job will actually rest on the answers to one or more of these questions, *do not* ask them until you have a written job offer in hand. There is still time to get the answers you want and may even need, but *now is not the time.* These kinds of questions are likely to hurt you more than help you at this point in the process.

GOOD QUESTIONS

If those are bad questions that may hurt you, what are some examples of good questions that may help you? Good questions showcase your knowledge and interest in the profession, job, or hiring organization. They also make you appear bright, inquisitive, proactive, educated, and focused on *them*, not *you*.

Remember in Tip 4 when we talked about doing your homework beforehand? In that chapter, you learned the importance of preparing for the interview by familiarizing yourself with the hiring organization and the position you are seeking. You'll recall that this can be done by scouring the Internet for the organization's websites, publications, annual reports, news articles, history, organizational charts, performance history, mission, vision, core values, and so on. This process also involves studying the position description and practicing ahead of time.

Leveraging what you learned from doing your homework can also help you formulate good questions, as shown in the examples below.

EXAMPLE 9–2

Let's look at an example using a fictitious publishing company named Write On. Suppose you are interested in an editor position at the company. When doing your homework before the interview, you find that the company is expanding its editorial services to include an online editing tool for both end users and in-house editors. Your research also shows that the company intends to continue its expansion across the globe: it plans to open offices in Asia next year, where its major competitor, the equally fictitious Publishing Inc., already has a foothold. Finally, your research shows that the company's vision is to bring the written word to every nation on earth. With that in mind, consider the following question.

INTERVIEWER QUESTION
Do you have any questions for me?

YOUR ANSWER
Yes, thank you. I recently read that Write On, in keeping with its vision, is planning to expand to Asia next year. Do you anticipate that the company will establish its presence in Shanghai, like Publishing Inc. has done, or does Write On anticipate another Asian market to be more advantageous, particularly since China's economy has taken a recent downturn?

INSIDE THE MIND OF THE INTERVIEWER
Even if you are only mildly interested in the answer to this question, can you see how it may serve you well, due to what it leads your interviewer to think about your character, competence, and chemistry/compatibility? Let's explore that by going inside the mind of the interviewer.

Interviewer's Question: *Do you have any questions for me?*

Your Answer:
Yes, thank you. I recently read that Write On, in keeping with its vision, is planning to expand to Asia next year. Do you anticipate that the company will establish its presence in Shanghai, like Publishing Inc. has done, or does Write On anticipate another Asian market to be more advantageous, particularly since China's economy has taken a recent downturn?

Interviewer's Thoughts		
Character	**Competence**	**Chemistry/Compatibility**
It's clear that this candidate has really done his/her homework. I'm pleased to see his/her preparedness and intellectual curiosity.	This candidate is well-read. He/she obviously stays current on world news and is knowledgeable about the economy and world markets.	This kind of proactive and informed person would be interesting to work with and be a good stimulus and example to others on the team.
He/she is taking this job seriously and seems sincerely interested in our company, what it stands for, and its future.	This candidate is also knowledgeable about our company, its vision, and its business plan.	

WHAT DO YOU THINK?

What do you think about the quality of this question? Who is that question about—*you* or *them*? How did your question show that you did your homework beforehand? How did your question influence the interviewer's perceptions of your character, competence, and chemistry/compatibility?

_____

_____

_____

_____

MORE EXAMPLES OF GOOD QUESTIONS

Other good questions for this organization and scenario might include the following:

- *Write On already has a strong presence in North America and Europe and is planning to establish a presence in Asia next year. Given its vision of serving the whole world, does Write On plan to enter the South American and Australian markets in the near or longer terms?*
- *I read in Write On's recent annual report that 50 percent of the company's annual revenues are currently derived from in-person editorial services and the other 50 percent from publishing margins. Does Write On expect the advent of its new online editing tool to significantly shift the revenue balance?*

For additional examples of good questions, let's use another scenario. Suppose you are interviewing for a teaching job in a nearby school district. In that case, good questions would demonstrate your knowledge of that school district, the education profession, and any factors that lead to student success. These questions might include the following:

- *What strategies does this district employ for parent involvement?*
- *How do you utilize formative and summative assessments in this district?*
- *I read that this district recently received a technology grant. To what extent will that grant allow technology to be available and used for student achievement?*

Again, you can see how good questions showcase your knowledge of the organization or profession, as well as your proactivity in doing your homework ahead of time. They demonstrate your interest in the hiring organization and the job you are applying for, and they reflect well on you as a candidate.

NOW YOU TRY IT!

Now that you've got the idea of both good and bad questions to ask or avoid asking during an interview, try creating a couple of good and bad questions of your own. Pick a real or fictitious organization and scenario, and research (or create) a little background information to help you formulate your questions. Jot down the organization and scenario below, as well as your examples of good and bad questions.

ORGANIZATION AND SCENARIO

_____
_____
_____
_____

GOOD QUESTIONS

1. _____
   _____

2. _____
   _____

BAD QUESTIONS

1. _____
   _____

2. _____
   _____

WHAT DO YOU THINK?

How do you think you did with your sample questions? How do you think your good questions would reflect well on you during an interview? How do you think your bad questions would reflect poorly?

_____
_____
_____
_____

SUMMARY: TIP 9

Toward the end of most interviews, interviewers often ask if you have any questions you would like to ask them. You should always take advantage of that opportunity and be prepared to ask two or three good questions. Knowing the difference between good and bad questions is vital.

Bad questions can actually hurt your image and your candidacy. As you now know, until you have a written job offer in hand, you are the seller (selling yourself as the product), and the interviewer is the buyer. Bad questions (such as asking about vacations, benefits, or promotions) ask about what *they* can do for *you*. Bad questions also indicate doubts, conditions, or worries that you may have about taking the job.

Good questions can help you appear intelligent and educated and like someone who has proactively done his/her homework beforehand. Leveraging what you learned from your homework can help you formulate questions that showcase your knowledge and interest in the organization or position (such as the organization's products or growth plans or the position responsibilities). Asking these good questions makes you more attractive as a candidate.

Try Not to Discuss Salary
If You Can Avoid It

By "discussing salary," I mean suggesting the dollar amount you should be paid in the new position if your interviewer asks you about that during the interview process. Any salary discussions and negotiations (if required) should ideally take place after you receive a written offer. (See the epilogue for further information.) Although it is not always feasible to avoid current or future salary discussions during the interview process, if at all possible, try not to offer up your salary requirements. The reason to avoid discussing salary during the interview process is that you do not want to risk "negotiating against yourself" if you can help it.

As you know by now, you are the seller (selling yourself as the product), and the interviewer is the buyer. This is the situation until you get a written offer, at which point you switch roles. As the buyer, an interviewer already has a good idea of how much he/she is willing to "spend" on you. Like any buyer, an interviewer doesn't usually want to pay more than that amount but would often like to pay less if given the opportunity. Conversely, an interviewee who has a salary requirement that is higher than an interviewer/buyer is willing to spend may not receive a job offer. Either way, it is important to try not to discuss salary during the interview process if you can avoid it, as you may put yourself at risk of getting a lower salary offer (or no offer at all).

For example, suppose an interviewer is willing to "buy" you for up to $100,000 in annual base salary, and the interviewer asks you (the seller) how much salary you require. What if you respond that the interviewer can buy you (the product) for $60,000 in annual base salary? What would he/she think? And what salary do you think the interviewer would offer you? Probably not the $100,000 he/she was willing to offer. And who put the $60,000 price tag on your head? You did.

On the other hand, let's assume a company's salary range for the position you are applying for is $80,000–$100,000 and that you are currently making $90,000. Suppose you know that you would accept an offer that was between $90,000 and $100,000, but you decide to aim high and say that you require a minimum of $110,000 when asked what salary you are looking for. If the company is bound by the limits of the salary range, you may have just talked yourself out of the running for this position, even though you might have accepted an offer that fell within the salary range. In order to avoid these traps, try not to state any salary requirements if at all possible.

Still, it is not always feasible to avoid salary discussions during the interview process; many application forms actually require you to state your current salary requirements. Some recruiters or screeners will not allow you to proceed to the next step of the interview process without first discussing salary. If that happens, just remember that your current salary does not necessarily dictate your new salary. Also remember that you can still negotiate salary, if necessary, after you receive a written offer and you know that they want you for the position. (This is because, at that point, you become the buyer, and they become the seller.)

Finally, know your own mind about your salary requirements before the interview, and do some homework on competitive salaries in your field. Assuming such information is available, find out what the hiring organization pays for similar positions.

For example, if you are making $75,000 per year in your current job and your research tells you that similar jobs in the market (and in the new organization) pay in the $80,000–$100,000 per year range, you want to have that knowledge as you enter the interview process. Still, if possible, you should avoid stating your salary requirements until you receive a written offer.

EXAMPLE 10-1

In order to put this all together, let's use an example of how to handle a salary-related question, based on the above scenario. Suppose you currently make $75,000 in annual base salary, and you had to put that on your application when applying for a job at the fictitious XYZ Company. Your preinterview research also told you that the going rate for these positions in the marketplace is $80,000–$100,000 per year; you also have colleagues in XYZ Company who make at least that much. During the interview, the interviewer begins to discuss salary requirements with you, as follows.

INTERVIEWER'S QUESTION

I see from your application that you make seventy-five thousand dollars a year at your current position. What sort of salary would you be looking for in this position?

YOUR ANSWER

If I were privileged enough to receive an offer from XYZ Company, I would seriously consider any offer that is competitive with the current market for these positions.

ALTERNATE ANSWER
I'd like to increase my current salary by at least five thousand dollars.

WHAT DO YOU THINK?
What thoughts about your new salary do you think these answers would trigger in the mind of the interviewer? What salary amount do you think the interviewer would consider, based on the first answer? The alternate answer? If the salary range for these positions at XYZ Company was $80,000–$100,000, where in the salary range do you think you would be likely to receive an offer if you provided the first answer? And if you provided the alternate answer?

_____

_____

_____

_____

SUMMARY: TIP 10
Salary discussions and negotiations (if required) should ideally take place only after you receive a written offer. If you are the first person to offer a salary suggestion during an interview, you risk being put in a position where you are inadvertently negotiating against yourself. The interviewer (buyer) knows how much he/she is willing to pay and may seize an opportunity to pay you less than he/she had in mind if you propose a lower salary than that figure. Conversely, if you state a salary requirement that is too high, you may rob yourself of a job offer that may be a little lower than that but that is still acceptable to you.

It is not always possible to avoid salary discussions during the interview process; many applications actually request that you state your current salary. Some recruiters or screeners will not allow you to proceed to the next step of the interview process without discussing your salary requirements. If this happens, just remember that your current salary does not necessarily dictate your new salary. Also remember that you can still negotiate salary, if necessary, after you receive a written offer and you know that they want you for the position. (This is because at that point, you become the buyer, and they become the seller.)

Finally, know your own mind about your salary requirements before the interview starts, and do some homework on competitive salaries in your field—as well as what the hiring organization pays for similar positions if that information is available.

Epilogue

What Happens When the Interview Is Over?

The last thing you should do before you leave your interview, and the first thing you should do when you get home, is to say "thank you." As you leave your interview, your thank you is in person. When you get home from your interview, your thank you is in writing. This can be accomplished by e-mail or a handwritten note mailed through the postal service. The advantage of e-mail is its expediency, which is especially helpful if the candidate selection process is likely to happen quickly.

A postinterview thank-you note should be short, sweet, and professional in tone. It should begin with you thanking the interviewer for his/her time and the opportunity to meet with him/her. It should state how even more enthused and interested you are after exploring the position and discussing the degree to which your background and experience match the company's requirements. Finally, the note should express your heightened desire to contribute to the interviewer's organization and that you look forward to hearing from him/her. That's about it—and it usually can be accomplished in three or four short sentences. Then, you wait. With any luck, before too long the organization will let you know, one way or another.

WHAT IF YOU RECEIVE AN OFFER?

If you do receive a job offer, it can be delivered in person, via telephone, and/or in writing (e-mail or otherwise). Once you receive the offer, the first thing you should do (the next time you communicate with the sender) is to say thank you. It is a great compliment to receive a job offer, and it should be treated as such by a sincere expression of gratitude.

If the offer is presented verbally (in person or via telephone), try not to accept, reject, or negotiate the offer until you have the offer in writing. Most importantly, do not resign from your current position until you have the offer in writing. This is because most verbal offers are not binding. It is difficult to prove an offer was made unless it is in some kind of written form (letter, e-mail, etc.)

Note: Even if you have a written offer, do not discuss it with your current employer until you have decided to accept the offer, as it may put your current job in jeopardy.

If you receive a verbal offer, in addition to saying thank you, ask when you might be able to receive the offer in writing—and do so without accepting or rejecting the offer. You may say something like, "Thank you. I am delighted to hear this and honored to have been selected. Could you give me a sense of when I might be able to receive the offer in writing? I am eager to review the offer and look forward to receiving it." Most organizations provide written offers as a matter of procedure. There are a few exceptions, but many of those organizations will provide a written offer upon request.

As stated numerous times throughout this book, once you receive a written offer, you and the interviewer change roles. Whereas you were the seller and the interviewer was the buyer during the interview process, after you receive a written offer you change roles: you become the buyer and the interviewer becomes the seller. The hiring organization has decided that you are the candidate of choice for *them*, and they now want to convince you to accept their offer. Now is the time for you to seriously consider whether or not the job is a match for *you*—and if it is what *you* want. Is it a good character, competence, and chemistry/compatibility match for *you*? If you are unsure at this point, now is the time to gather more information or to conduct any negotiations that might help with your decision.

With a written offer in hand, you are finally in a negotiating position (if necessary), and you are also in a position to ask questions (again, if necessary) that are more about *you* than *them*. Try not to negotiate unless you really need to. As the old saying goes, "A bird in the hand is worth two in the bush." Your offer is a valuable gift. Try not to jeopardize the offer by challenging it too much, especially if it is unnecessary to do so.

If you do decide to negotiate, be careful not to inadvertently accept or reject the offer during the negotiation process. Once you accept an offer, the window for negotiation becomes closed; once you decline an offer, the offer may be off the table for good. Anything that can be perceived as rejecting an offer, including making a counteroffer, may potentially eliminate your option to accept the original offer if you still want to do so after the negotiation process is concluded.

The best way to negotiate or ask questions without accepting or rejecting an offer is to *ask for clarification* or *additional information*. The way *not* to negotiate is to threaten or give ultimatums. For example, consider the following differences between these two negotiation strategies about paid vacations.

Negotiation Strategy 1: *I see in your letter that the offer includes two weeks of paid vacation. I have had three weeks of paid vacation for the past five years; I was wondering if it would be possible to have the same amount in this position.*

Negotiation Strategy 2: *I see in your letter that the offer includes two weeks of paid vacation. I have not had less than three weeks of paid vacation for the last five years, and I cannot accept an offer with a company that does not provide me with at least that much.*

Do you see the difference in these two strategies? The first positions the question about vacation as a request for more information and does not state that the offer will be rejected if the answer does not come back favorably. The second positions the request as a demand and clearly states that the offer will be rejected if the demand is not met.

Suppose the new company's representative replies that he/she cannot offer more than two weeks of paid vacation to new employees due to policy, precedence, and/or equity issues. If you use the first strategy, you can continue the discussion with the company and still accept their offer if you so desire. If you use the second strategy, you may inadvertently close the door on the offer.

The same is true for salary negotiations. Note the differences between the two strategies below.

Negotiation Strategy 1: *I see that you are offering me seventy thousand dollars as a base salary. I am currently making seventy thousand dollars per year, and I will not leave my current job for less than a ten percent increase.*

Negotiation Strategy 2: *I see that the offer includes seventy thousand dollars as a base salary. My current salary is equivalent to that, and I was hoping to realize more of a differential in a new position. Is there any flexibility in that regard?*

Again, do you see the difference in these two strategies? The first is stated as a threat, which, if not met, will result in a refusal of the offer and the closing of the conversation. The second strategy is a request for more information; even if the potential employer does not respond to it in the desired manner, posing the question in this way allows for the offer to remain on the table and for discussions to continue.

In short, for any question you may want to ask or anything you may need to negotiate after you receive a written offer, remember to position your questions in terms of a request for clarification or additional information. Do not use language that indicates acceptance or rejection of the offer until you have all the information you need.

On the other hand, if something is truly a deal-breaker and a "must-have" for you to accept a position, you can say so politely if the answer you receive to your request for information presents an insurmountable obstacle for you. For example, suppose you are a divorced parent who is only allowed to have custody of your children during the month of July. Let's say the job you have been offered involves significant international travel and that you are resolute about not accepting a job with any company that requires you to travel outside of the country during the month of July. In that case, you would ask about that in your request for information after receiving a written offer. (Remember, this kind of question should not be asked during the interview process—only after you receive a written offer.)

If the person you ask says that he/she is unsure if the company can make that commitment, you can say at that point (because it is true) that, although you would be heartbroken to do so, you would have to turn the offer down unless both parties can agree that you will not travel overseas during the month of July. Even if the answer still comes back as no and you end up having to turn down the offer, there is no real choice in a case like this, and the risk has to be taken. But it was worth asking, since there was the possibility that the employer could have granted your request.

Finally, once your negotiations (if necessary) are concluded, make sure to get the revised offer in writing again. If the original offer is the only written offer of record, the revisions agreed to during the negotiation process may be forgotten, misinterpreted, or disputed over time.

WHAT IF YOU DO NOT RECEIVE AN OFFER?

If you receive word that you did not get the position, again, say thank you. A short note or conversation that expresses gratitude for the opportunity to be considered and for the interviewer's time when you *don't* get an offer speaks even more loudly and positively about your character than a thank you expressed when you *do* get an offer.

You may also want to ask for feedback or suggestions on how you can improve in the future. If you choose to do this, ensure that you make the request in a humble manner, and make it clear that you are asking for the purposes of personal growth and development. You do not want to have your question misinterpreted as a request for the interviewer to justify his/her decision.

Thanking your interviewer and asking for developmental feedback tends to leave a favorable and lasting impression in the interviewer's mind about you as a person and a candidate. This may serve you well over the course of time, particularly if another position in that organization opens up in the future.

CLOSING THOUGHTS

Through the examples presented in this book, I have hoped to convey the idea that the person who has the most power to influence the interviewer's perception of you is *you*. Assuming you have the basic qualifications for the job you are applying for, how you handle yourself in an interview can make or break the interviewer's decision to hire you.

An interviewer's image of you before you enter the room is a fairly blank canvas, informed up to that point only by your résumé. You paint the rest of that picture by how you dress, how you act, what you say, and how you say it. All that interviewers really know about you is what you tell them. Therefore, your self-portrait—and your job—are in your hands. It is my sincere hope that the essential tips in this book will make those "hands" more skillful and give you the confidence and ability to help you land the job you want. I wish you much success!

10 ESSENTIAL TIPS SUMMARY

1. Know What Interviewers Are Looking (and Listening) For

2. Understand Behavioral Event Interviewing

3. Realize That It's Not All about You

4. Do Your Homework

5. Tell Your Story Well, Part A: Be Concise

6. Tell Your Story Well, Part B: Highlight Key Messages

7. Tell Your Story Well, Part C: Accentuate the Positive, and Eliminate the Negative

8. Tell Your Story Well, Part D: Mind Your Attitude

9. Ask Good Questions—and Don't Ask Bad Ones

10. Try Not to Discuss Salary If You Can Avoid It

Appendix A: Sample Interview Questions

SAMPLE INTERVIEW QUESTIONS

1. Why do you want this job?

2. Why should we hire you?

3. What would you like to gain or learn from this assignment?

4. What strengths or skills do you have that would help us develop this department?

5. Tell us about a time when you were faced with conflicting priorities. How did you determine your top priority?

6. Describe a project where you had to use project management skills.

7. Tell us about a project where you had to use organizational skills.

8. Describe a situation in which you improved a work procedure or process.

9. Tell us about your most relevant work experience.

10. What are your greatest strengths?

11. What do you consider to be your weaknesses?

12. What is your greatest professional achievement to date?

13. Tell me about a challenge or conflict you've faced at work and how you dealt with it. What happened as a result of this action?

14. Where do you see yourself in five years?

15. What is your dream job?

16. Why are you leaving your current job?

17. What are you looking for in a new position?

18. Tell me about a time you exercised leadership. What did you do? How did it turn out?

19. Tell me about a time you disagreed with a decision that was made at work.

20. How would your current boss and coworkers describe you?

21. Can you explain why you changed jobs—or career paths?

22. How have you dealt with high-pressure situations?

23. What are your salary requirements?

24. What are your goals?

25. Tell me about a time when you were most satisfied in your job.

26. What can you do for us that other candidates can't?

27. What are three positive things your last boss would say about you?

28. What are three negative things your last boss would say about you?

29. Describe a time when you had to work in a team situation.

30. Do you have any questions for me?

Appendix B: Practice Templates

PRACTICE TEMPLATE

Insert a question from Appendix A or one of your own in the "Interviewer's Question" section of the template below. Then practice (with a friend, if possible) by answering the question in the "Your Answer" section. Next, go inside the mind of the interviewer and capture what you and/or a friend think the interviewer's thoughts would be about your character, competence, and chemistry/compatibility based on your answer. Finally, reflecting on your answer and the interviewer's thoughts, describe how you think you did in the "What Do You Think?" section below.

Interviewer's Question:		
Your Answer:		
Interviewer's Thoughts		
Character	Competence	Chemistry/Compatibility

WHAT DO YOU THINK?

How do you think you did with your answer? How favorable (or unfavorable) of a self-portrait did you create in the interviewer's mind, based on how your answer depicted your character, competence, and chemistry/compatibility?

_____

_____

_____

_____

PRACTICE TEMPLATE

Insert a question from Appendix A or one of your own in the "Interviewer's Question" section of the template below. Then practice (with a friend, if possible) by answering the question in the "Your Answer" section. Next, go inside the mind of the interviewer and capture what you and/or a friend think the interviewer's thoughts would be about your character, competence, and chemistry/compatibility based on your answer. Finally, reflecting on your answer and the interviewer's thoughts, describe how you think you did in the "What Do You Think?" section below.

Interviewer's Question:		
Your Answer:		
Interviewer's Thoughts		
Character	**Competence**	**Chemistry/Compatibility**

WHAT DO YOU THINK?

How do you think you did with your answer? How favorable (or unfavorable) of a self-portrait did you create in the interviewer's mind, based on how your answer depicted your character, competence, and chemistry/compatibility?

_____

_____

_____

_____

PRACTICE TEMPLATE

Insert a question from Appendix A or one of your own in the "Interviewer's Question" section of the template below. Then practice (with a friend, if possible) by answering the question in the "Your Answer" section. Next, go inside the mind of the interviewer and capture what you and/or a friend think the interviewer's thoughts would be about your character, competence, and chemistry/compatibility based on your answer. Finally, reflecting on your answer and the interviewer's thoughts, describe how you think you did in the "What Do You Think?" section below.

Interviewer's Question:		
Your Answer:		
	Interviewer's Thoughts	
Character	**Competence**	**Chemistry/Compatibility**

WHAT DO YOU THINK?

How do you think you did with your answer? How favorable (or unfavorable) of a self-portrait did you create in the interviewer's mind, based on how your answer depicted your character, competence, and chemistry/compatibility?

_____

_____

_____

_____

PRACTICE TEMPLATE

Insert a question from Appendix A or one of your own in the "Interviewer's Question" section of the template below. Then practice (with a friend, if possible) by answering the question in the "Your Answer" section. Next, go inside the mind of the interviewer and capture what you and/or a friend think the interviewer's thoughts would be about your character, competence, and chemistry/compatibility based on your answer. Finally, reflecting on your answer and the interviewer's thoughts, describe how you think you did in the "What Do You Think?" section below.

Interviewer's Question:		
Your Answer:		
	Interviewer's Thoughts	
Character	**Competence**	**Chemistry/Compatibility**

WHAT DO YOU THINK?

How do you think you did with your answer? How favorable (or unfavorable) of a self-portrait did you create in the interviewer's mind, based on how your answer depicted your character, competence, and chemistry/compatibility?

_____

_____

_____

_____

PRACTICE TEMPLATE

Insert a question from Appendix A or one of your own in the "Interviewer's Question" section of the template below. Then practice (with a friend, if possible) by answering the question in the "Your Answer" section. Next, go inside the mind of the interviewer and capture what you and/or a friend think the interviewer's thoughts would be about your character, competence, and chemistry/compatibility based on your answer. Finally, reflecting on your answer and the interviewer's thoughts, describe how you think you did in the "What Do You Think?" section below.

Interviewer's Question:		
Your Answer:		
Interviewer's Thoughts		
Character	**Competence**	**Chemistry/Compatibility**

WHAT DO YOU THINK?

How do you think you did with your answer? How favorable (or unfavorable) of a self-portrait did you create in the interviewer's mind, based on how your answer depicted your character, competence, and chemistry/compatibility?

_____

_____

_____

_____

3

Made in the USA
Lexington, KY
07 March 2016